WHEN GOD SHOWS UP

A JOURNEY WITH GOD
THROUGH INCREDIBLE HIGHS
AND DEVASTATING LOWS.

BY SHARON WITHERSPOON

ISBN: 9781657375178

Independently Published

Illustrations by Sharon Witherspoon. Cover photo taken by the Paint Horse Journal. Author/Illustrator purchased rights to image from Larry Williams Photography who sold the rights on behalf of the Paint Horse Journal.

To Momma and Daddy

Thank you for always believing in me.

I am grateful you encourage me to be who God created me to be and to chase the dreams He has given me. Thank you for teaching me His ways, not just through His Word, but through your lives as well.

I am so blessed that He gave me you as my parents and as my friends.

With all my love,

Sharon

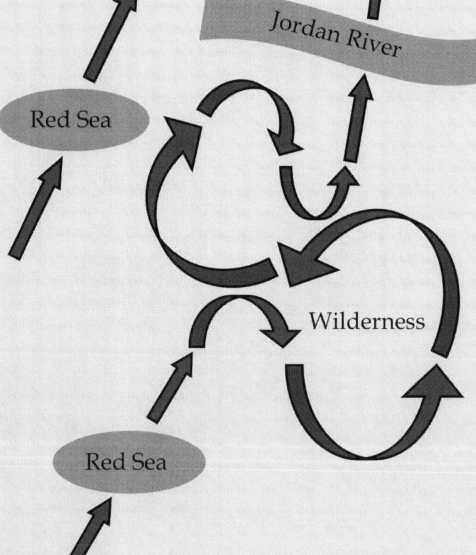

Table of Contents

A Letter to You, the Reader..7

The Red Sea

Chasing God-Sized Dreams...10

The Dream Continues...29

The Wilderness

The Dream Deferred...38

God's Grace..50

God's Presence..60

Preparation..70

God's Perspective of Us..80

Purpose..90

God's Perspective of Our Circumstances...................................105

Provision..118

Protection..132

Perseverance..145

The Jordan River

Pressing On..164

Parting Waters...175

The Promised Land

"As for me and my horse, we will serve the LORD."................186

To God Be the Glory...203

Photos..218

Notes...250

Dear Reader,

While this book is a testimony of how God has moved and worked in my life, my prayer is that the lessons I have learned will somehow help you with your journey with Him. Therefore, feel free to write in this book like you would a Bible study workbook. Highlight points that resonate with you. If you do not agree with something, feel free to make note of what you believe instead. You will not hurt my feelings any. Your faith should be your own, not a carbon-copy, cookie cutter version of mine. This book is meant to make you think, to grow, and to assist you in deepening your faith and in solidifying what you truly believe.

Therefore, before every chapter, I have included additional verses to help summarize the spiritual lessons that follow. At the end of every chapter are "Points to Ponder" that give you the opportunity to apply what you have read to your own life and your own relationship with God. Blank space is included after every chapter for you to record your thoughts, journal prayers, draw, or however else you wish to use it. This book is more than just my story. It is His story, and, maybe, in a way, it is your story, too. So, make this book your own. Fill it with your own ideas, prayers, and dreams. Use it to help see how God shows up for you in your journey. I cannot wait to see how He does!

Love in Christ,
Sharon

My Plan

God's Plan

Promised Land

Promised Land

Jordan River

Red Sea

Red Sea

Wilderness

The Red Sea

"The LORD will fight for you; you need only to be still."

Exodus 14:14

Chapter 1

Chasing God-sized Dreams

"The LORD himself goes before you and will be with you;
he will never leave you nor forsake you.
Do not be afraid; do not be discouraged."
Deuteronomy 31:8

"Thank you, exhibitors, bring your horses to the center and line up, please. Bring your horses to the center." At that moment, you realize your class is finished. You have done all you can do, and the results are now in God's hands. While you wait for the judges to tally their scores and finalize placings, you pray, and you reflect on the journey that brought you here, to the 2017 American Paint Horse Association (APHA) Open and Amateur World Championship Show, where you are currently showing in Amateur Solid Paint Bred Hunt Seat Equitation.

Our journey to World began many years ago. Growing up, I was as horse crazy as they came, and I dreamed of a horse of my own and of one day having a ranch where I could use horses to point people to God. I rode a pony for the first time when I was around five years old at the International Wildlife Park in Grand Prairie, Texas. Sitting on that pony's back was the greatest feeling in the world, and I loved it so much I begged my parents to let me ride a second time. I was hooked, and I began saving money for a horse of my own. I would read every book or magazine about horses that I could get my hands on. I wanted to learn all I could about these beautiful, athletic creatures.

In first grade, I came in from recess, and after a bit, I realized my heart had not slowed back down from running and playing. I told my teacher, who took my pulse and immediately ran to the office to call my parents. My heart eventually slowed back down on its own, but my life dramatically changed after that. Doctors' appointments. Holter monitors. Stress tests. All while still trying to be a normal kid. Even at a young age, I was competitive, and winning a race one year at Field Day gave me dreams running track, as well as playing basketball. All that changed, though, when I was diagnosed with tachycardia. I was put on beta blockers, which meant that when my body was triggered to produce adrenaline, it could not. I would be running, and it would be like hitting a wall. I knew there was so much more in the tank, so to speak, but no matter how hard I tried, I could not make my legs pump any faster. I went from being one of the fastest to one of the slowest, from being in the thick of things, to being one of the last picked. It was devastating. But then there were horses. Horses did not care that I had a heart condition. Horses never looked at me like there was something wrong with me. Like I was broken. They loved unconditionally, and they offered a freedom from the limits beta blockers put on me. How fast we went depended on their legs, not mine. How long and how far we would go depended on their stamina, not mine. I felt whole again when I sat on a horse's back.

Having a heart condition as a child gives you a perspective of your own mortality that most kids never have. With tachycardia, my heart would race so fast that it would not be pumping effectively. I was taught techniques to help it come back under control. The only way my heart would return to normal rhythm was by stopping and then restarting. Imagine being a child hooked up to an EKG and seeing yourself flat line. Both my mom and my dad felt my heart stop while they were taking my pulse during tachycardia episodes. It was not until I took Equine Exercise Physiology in college that I understood the biomechanics of the techniques I had been taught, and only then did I fully realize I had been taught how to stop my heart. Fortunately, with the type of tachycardia I had, my heart would always restart on its own, but knowing that was not the case for everyone made me appreciate the value of life and how fleeting it is, even as a child.

My strong, Christian parents gave me stability through this. They lived out their faith, trusting God and drawing upon His strength even when times were uncertain. My favorite verse as a child was, and is, Philippians 4:13 (NKJV), "I can do all things through Christ who strengthens me." When I went to the cardiologist for the first time and saw this in his office, it gave me comfort. I knew I could handle whatever lay ahead because Christ would give me the strength to do so. I also knew, though, being raised in church, that this life is not all there is. There is a life after this one, one that is either spent with God or spent separated from God. At eight years old, I knew that I needed to make sure that if things went wrong, if I died, I would go to Heaven to be with God. So, one Sunday, I went forward and told my pastor that I wanted to give my life to Jesus and be forgiven for my sins. The moment I did, a peace came over me, a peace beyond all explanation or understanding. In that moment I knew, no matter what the future held for me, my eternity with God was secure because of Christ, and that He would be with me, every step of the way.

During one tachycardia episode, the EMT caught on the EKG an irregularity that he recognized as a particular kind of tachycardia involving the electrical aspect of the heart. This caused me to get referred to an electrocardiologist who recommended a heart catheterization and ablation. The doctor would sever nerves in my heart that were causing it to short circuit. Sever the wrong one, and I would need a pacemaker. Momma later told me that after hearing this, she could not bring herself to pray for God's will to be done. She wanted me to be alright and knew sometimes God says no, and she could not bear that thought. She said she confided this to one of her cousins. He told her that was okay. God wants us to be honest with Him. Fall of my seventh grade year, I went into surgery. I was scared, but I knew my family and friends were praying for me, and God would be with me, just as He had every moment thus far. During the surgery the doctor severed, I believe, four nerves. Six weeks later I returned for a follow up where they severed one more. I was then released and was told once the incisions healed, I could return to normal activities. I was excited at the prospect of chasing those long ago shelved dreams of track and basketball; however, it had been so long since I had experienced adrenaline, it took time to figure out what normal was supposed to feel like. One coach was patient with me. One was not. I was told I was too far behind on my basketball skills. In a moment my dreams of being an athlete seemed to be gone, but God had other ideas.

While sports at school were off the table, horses were not. My family could not afford riding lessons, but I would go on trail rides at the lake nearby, and occasionally my dad's water well customers would let me ride their horses. I rode every chance I was given. I kept reading about horses, riding, and training, and kept saving money for a horse. However, I came to realize, as high school graduation approached, that boarding a horse while at college would be too expensive, so I decided to wait until after college to pursue my dream of owning a horse. God blessed, and somehow, I was good enough of a rider to make the Intercollegiate Horse Show Association western riding team at Midway College, now Midway University, in Kentucky, complete with an NAIA athletic scholarship. I signed a letter of intent just like any other sport. God knew where my focus needed to be, and He removed the distractions of track and basketball so that I could focus on what He intended for me to do, pursue my passion with horses. At Midway I majored in equine studies and took both western and hunt seat riding courses. While in college, God continued to fan the flames of my childhood desire to use horses as a ministry tool, and working at a Baptist camp with their horses the summer of my senior year confirmed this calling on my life.

I first met my mare, Aria, when she was a foal on my cousins Pat and Debbie Moore's horse farm. She was absolutely adorable. A little Black Beauty, just a filly instead of a colt, and full of personality. Friendly. Loving. At the time, I did not even think of the possibility that she would end up being mine. We were just visiting my cousins, and they were letting me love on their horses. About a year later, as graduation approached, Pat and Debbie knew I was looking for a horse to buy. They told me they had one for me to consider. I came out to their place during Christmas break, and lo and behold, the horse they had in mind for me was Aria. She had grown and was even more beautiful, and though she was too young to ride, watching her move in the round pen, I could tell she was something special. When I decided she was the horse I wanted, another cousin of mine bought her for me as a college graduation present. Aria's dam (mother) is a Quarter Horse, and her sire (father) is a black and white tobiano Paint. The hope was that Aria would be a tobiano as well; however, she was born the spitting image of her dam, black with a white star. She could still be registered with APHA but as what was at that time called "Breeding Stock," now known as "Solid Paint Bred" or "SPB."

Aria is an incredible mare, very intelligent and still full of personality. She can be as sweet as can be, but she is also protective of me. She is willing to please and eager to learn. Any short comings we have had through the years have been due to me and my limitations as a rider and as her trainer, rather than any limitations on her part. Since she was two when I graduated college, I had the opportunity to start Aria from the ground up, teaching her ground manners, bonding with her, teaching her to submit in a round pen, her first saddling, her first ride, it was all up to me. Through this process, God began to show me how her learning to submit and follow my leading mirrors me learning to submit to Him and follow His leading. I realized then that He has plans to use Aria's and my journey together as a conduit to point people to Him, on what scale I am still not sure. Training Aria has been a joy. She is incredibly smooth to ride and will try her best to please. As long as I clearly communicate to her what I want, she will do her best to execute what I ask. With practice and patience, she has become very light and responsive, taking on both western and hunt seat disciplines.

Early in our show career together, we only went to local open shows, meaning anyone can attend, does not matter what breed your horse is. The dream of going to APHA World was there, but as the author Holley Gerth puts it so well, World was a God-sized dream that only He could accomplish[1], and one we were not ready to take on. Paint Horse folks from all over the nation and the world come to this show to square off and see who is the best in the world in each class. We were not that caliber yet. At open shows, we participated in western and hunt seat flat classes, as well as in over fences classes, which both Aria and I enjoyed. We took occasional lessons with Tracey Badley Walton at Spellbound Farm to help us both improve over fences. This gave Aria exposure to unique jumps and also gave her regular excursions away from home, building her confidence. However, after soundness issues cropped up due to jumping, our vet, Dr. Glenn Tolle, encouraged a career change, so I began considering options. I had recently learned of a new class that APHA offered called ranch pleasure, now known as ranch riding. The class is a pattern class that encourages natural, forward movement at all gaits. It sounded like something Aria and I could do, but I was not sure about taking on breed shows, meaning shows only open to one particular breed of horses. Breed shows are typically larger, more expensive, and offer stiffer competition due to horses being more specialized. After much prayer, God pointed me to Proverbs 21:31, which in NIV says, "The horse is made ready for the day of battle, but victory rests with the LORD." God impressed upon me that it is my job to do all I can to get Aria and I ready for horse shows, but the results are entirely up to Him, no matter how big or how small the show, and so, I stepped out on faith, and entered our first APHA show in 2014. Aria did well, in fact, really well. We won our class under both judges. God blessed our efforts and made it clear that we were on the path He had laid out for us.

Aria took to ranch riding quickly and thoroughly enjoyed it. We met some great, Godly folks at shows. One couple, Sam and Michelle Reding, invited me to bring Aria out to their place to ride in their arena. At home, Aria and I just rode out in the pasture, practicing patterns, visualizing an arena space to work in. This worked, but the opportunity to practice from time to time in an arena was a huge blessing. As we trained, we ran into issues with our lead changes; she would change smoothly from her right to left lead, but buck from left to right. Dr. Tolle checked her out to make sure there were no physical reasons for her behavior, and then he recommended contacting Mead McGee, a great horseman who both trains and does equine dentistry. After talking with Mead, he was more than willing to help us, and Sam and Michelle agreed for us to meet at their place for lessons. The more time I spent with Mead, the more I came to respect him, not just as a trainer, but as a man of God as well. He became not only our western trainer, but also a dear friend. With Mead's help, Aria and I gradually improved, not only with our lead changes, but with other aspects of ranch riding and our training in general.

We qualified for 2015 and 2016 World, and even though ranch riding was not offered either year for SPBs, we still attended and showed in Amateur SPB Hunter Under Saddle and Amateur SPB Hunt Seat Equitation both years. Our performances improved from one year to the next. Going to World felt a bit like a David and Goliath story. We were the underdogs going up against horses and riders who had much more experience and could afford much more training and lessons than we could, which made any placing a huge accomplishment. Our improvement bolstered my confidence, and I set my eyes on the 2017 World Championship Show. I had no clue how difficult the road ahead would be.

In 2005, my mom was diagnosed with pulmonary arterial hypertension, an incurable, progressive condition. Early on,

Momma would come out to shows and cheer me on. However, as her health declined, she was no longer strong enough to go, nor could she handle the dustiness of arenas. Instead, we began videoing my rides so that she could still be a part of everything. She would pray at home, and we would call in and report on how my classes went. As her condition progressed, her vision deteriorated as well. She was still able to see well enough to see the videos from 2016 World, but after that her vision got to the point she could not distinguish what was going on. She did not let that stop her though. She continued being a prayer warrior, not only for horse shows, but for our entire family and our friends. She could have let her condition make her bitter, but instead she chose to focus on the good and to focus on praying for the needs of others. Even though she could no longer see well enough to read God's Word, she stormed the throne room of God for family and friends. She knew so much of God's Word by heart and would remind us of His promises when we needed them the most. When her strength allowed, she also shared His Word through music, her beautiful voice bringing to life treasured hymns. Growing up, our home was filled with music, from both her singing and her playing the piano, gifts she also shared at church. I have found sometimes God can speak just as clearly through music as He can through His Word.

The summer prior to the 2016 World Show, my beloved dog, Blue, had been diagnosed with liver cancer. Blue was an incredibly smart, very athletic, husky/shepherd mix with an uncanny ability to bring joy and love to any situation. I got her when she was just a puppy while I was living in an apartment in Dallas. She had perfect husky, almost wolf-like, markings as a puppy, dark widow's peak, back, and ruff-like collar, white face, chest, belly, and legs. Once while I was taking her on a walk, some kids hollered at me asking if I got her from the zoo. She loved her family, whom she would herd around the house from time to time, and acted like a furry human, from her facial expressions to her sounding like she spoke words. She loved to play and loved to cuddle. She gave me unconditional love and companionship. Her favorite word was "go" and would get beside herself with excitement when asked if she wanted to go on a truck ride, sometimes even having to run laps in the house before she would stop to put her harness on. She also had incredible tracking skills, even as a pup. Daddy took her on a walk the first time I brought her home, and he told her "ok, Blue, it's time to go back inside." She put her nose to the ground and retraced her steps all the way to the front door. God gave her this keen nose because He knew she would need it to help Momma.

When Momma first went onto oxygen, Blue was just two years old. We were worried how Blue would behave around it. Turned out we had nothing to be concerned about. She was a self-taught service dog who would use her keen nose and ears to detect leaks in Momma's oxygen line, affectionately dubbed "Squiggles," and fuss at Momma if she took her oxygen off for very long. Blue would nap on Squiggles so that she could always keep up with Momma. If Momma moved, Squiggles would move, and Blue would wake up and follow her wherever she went in the house. Blue's diagnosis hit all of us hard, and after 2016 World, both her and Momma's health declined greatly. After the first of the year, Momma was in and out of the hospital, each time seemly a little weaker than before she went in. She was put on 15L of oxygen, which is an incredibly large amount, and at times it still was not enough. As her vision continued to deteriorate, she was incredibly grateful for Blue's markings, which had changed as she grew, white paws fading to gold legs, white face, gold head, blue body, white plume tail, for they helped her show up on the grey carpet. Blue was not able to get up quickly anymore, so she could not get out of the way if Momma did not see her in time. Blue passed away March 23, 2017. Her passing left a huge hole in my heart, for she was my "fur baby." Momma told me that her prayer had been that she would still be with us when Blue passed away so that she could be there to comfort me.

During Momma's hospital stays, she always made a point to pray for chaplains when they came to pray for her. She made comment that "Prayer is hope laid at the feet of Jesus." During one stay, I found us matching necklaces at Lifeway that were inscribed with her favorite verse, Deuteronomy 31:8, "The LORD himself goes before you and will be with you; he will never leave you nor forsake you. Do not be afraid; do not be discouraged." She loved that verse, not only because it was a reminder that God is with us, but also that He goes ahead of us. There is nothing that we face, nothing that lies ahead of us, that He does not already have a plan to handle. He is already there before we even get there. That is why we have no reason to fear. Momma leaned on this verse heavily. She knew God was with her, and not only with her, but He was going ahead of her, leading the way. She took comfort in the fact that He was doing the same for our family, that He would be with us, going ahead of us, into the uncertain days ahead. Momma never had the chance to wear her necklace. She passed away June 13, 2017. It was the hardest day of my life. Momma was my best friend, and I did not have Blue waiting at home to bury my face in her fur and breathe in her comfort. Daddy and I went home from the hospital to an empty house. It was so quiet. No oxygen concentrators running. No happy to see us barks and yips. The next day, Daddy and I went out to the barn to feed Aria. Normally, Aria at feeding time is all about her food, whinnying and nickering, encouraging me to get her breakfast to her as fast as possible. That day was different. That day she walked right up to Daddy and hung her head low, bowing in grief, offering her sympathy to him. It was so moving and so beautiful. Somehow, she knew Momma had passed, and she was sharing in our sorrow.

We had already qualified for 2017 World before Momma had passed away. She knew we had qualified, and she was proud and excited for us. Even though it would be hard, Daddy and I decided to still go to World. It is what Momma would have wanted. She would not have wanted her passing to cause me to give up on my dreams. The choice was clear. It was time to buckle down and train hard. By this time Sam and Michelle had sold their place and moved a couple hours away, so I no longer had a place to meet

Mead for lessons. Ranch riding for solids had been added to the classes offered at APHA World, but I still wanted to show in the hunt seat classes we had shown in previously. To do well, to have a performance that would honor God, as well as Momma's memory, I knew I needed lessons to do everything possible to get Aria ready for "battle." I contacted Tracey at Spellbound Farm, where we had taken jumper lessons, and she and her assistant, Kayla Larson, began working with us on our hunt seat equitation. Once the patterns for World were posted, we began practicing and polishing each and every part. I still knew, though, that the only way we would do well at World was if God showed up and moved in a mighty way. I clung to both Proverbs 21:31 and Deuteronomy 31:8. The first is emblazoned on Aria's stall sign, and I wore the necklace of the other everyday as a reminder that God was going ahead of us, envisioning Him going before us into the arena at World. My prayer was that we would show the world what happens when God shows up.

Leading up to World, I began working and praying my way through Priscilla Shirer's study on the armor of God[2]. I knew that when I made World about pointing people to God, spiritual warfare would ignite, and I needed to be prepared. Sure enough, the closer World got, the more heated the attacks became. My prayers adapted to include Exodus 14:14, "The LORD will fight for you; you need only to be still." I asked that He handle the attacks and that He continually remind me of His truth and His promises. Aria too seemed to feel the onslaught. She, like Blue, has an uncanny ability to detect moods and emotions, and her behavior responds accordingly. When we arrived in Fort Worth for World, she was a bundle of nerves and energy. Fortunately, God, as promised, was ahead of us, and Aria and I were selected to go first in Amateur SPB Hunt Seat Equitation, which meant no time standing around waiting that could easily translate into nervous meltdowns on both our parts.

Aria and I confidently walked to the cone, pausing for the flag that signaled we were to begin. We struck off at the trot and executed our pattern. We rode the pattern as precisely as we could, and I held my posture as correctly possible for equitation. Our lines were straight, our corners square, our circle round, our transitions sharp, our number of steps accurate, our back solid. When we exited the arena, I knew we had done our best, but I also knew that we had performed the pattern even better during practice. Aria had leg yielded a little in our simple change, and her pivot foot moved slightly in our turn on the forehand, something that had never happened in practice. The results were very much in God's hands at this point. After everyone in the class had completed their patterns, we were called back into the arena to work along the rail as a group. This gives the judges the opportunity to break any ties or tweak their placings. At the conclusion, we were asked to line up in the center of the arena to await their decisions.

While I waited, I began praying yet again that God would bless our efforts, praying that we at least not be last. I thought about Daddy being up in the stands watching and how hard it had been on both of us not being able to call Momma and report on how things were going. I envisioned Momma and Blue and the rest of our family in Heaven all gathered around, watching our class, cheering us on. The placings then began. They always start at the bottom of the placings and work their way up, which adds an air of suspense. Fifth place was announced…not me…ok good…at least I am not last…fourth place…not me…oh wow! That means I am in the top three! Tears begin to flow…third place…still not me…tears begin a bit heavier because I realize that this means I am either Reserve or World Champion…Reserve is announced…not…me… At this point I cannot hold the tears back at all. Aria and I had done it! God had granted us the God-sized dream He had given us! We, the underdogs, had just WON A WORLD CHAMPIONSHIP!! When they announced our number, Aria knew she had done well. I bent over and gave her a kiss on the neck and a hug. She proudly trotted up to the woman who was handing out the awards. I was crying and smiling from ear to ear. When the woman told me congratulations, and put the neck ribbon on Aria, I told her that Momma had passed away this summer and that was why this was so special. She looked up at me with tears in her eyes, and said, "your mom had the best seat in the house today." They then brought up the music for our victory gallop, and the tears just flowed, for the song they were playing was "You Raise Me Up" by Josh Groban.[3] No one in APHA knew about Momma. They had just randomly picked that song, but the choice was inspired by God to let me know that Momma saw, that she was proud, and that both she and He was there in that moment with us.

"When I am down and oh my soul so weary, When troubles come and my heart burdened be, Then I am still and wait here in the silence Until you come and sit a while with me. You raise me up, so I can stand on mountains. You raise me up, to walk on stormy seas. I am strong, when I am on your shoulders. You raise me up, to more than I can be."[3]

2017 had been a year of loss. My heart had been burdened, and my soul had been weary. However, God came along side me, alongside my family. He sat with us, grieved with us, and then He raised us up to more than what we could be on our own. We could not have won a World Championship without Him. He did this. Not us. He did this so that we could point people to Him. This, ladies and gentlemen, is what happens when God shows up! God-sized dreams come true when God moves in a mighty way! So whatever dream you have that is too big to accomplish on your own, that you know beyond a shadow of a doubt that God gave you, keep working towards that dream. Keep preparing that horse for battle, and leave the results in God's hands. In His time, He will show up. He will work in a mighty way. That God-sized dream of yours will come true. Just like mine did.

The show was not over yet though…

Points to Ponder...

- What dream has God given you that seems too big to be possible? What are some ways you feel God is asking you to step out in faith and pursue this dream?

- How have you seen God show up in your own life? What mighty works has He accomplished on your behalf?

- How has God shown you He is with you and going before you in both good times and in difficult times? How has that encouraged you?

Chapter 2

The Dream Continues

"I can do all things through Christ who strengthens me."
Philippians 4:13 (NKJV)

We returned to World a week after our World Championship to compete in Open SPB Ranch Riding, the class that started our career of APHA shows. Because the class was "Open," that meant we would be not only competing against amateurs like myself, but also professional horse trainers. I had struggled with whether or not to enter. Being the inaugural year for the class, there was no separate amateur class and no assurance of one the next year. I knew several of the riders who were entering the class, one being my dear friend Cherie Bugg. She had the same concerns as mine about showing against professionals, but upon her encouragement, I entered. Aria and I have always fallen short in this class as the competition has intensified over the years, but we would go have fun and cheer our friends on.

Almost all of our training, and definitely all our lessons, leading up to World were hunt seat, so I attended a ranch show a couple of weeks prior to World to get some practice in. Part of the pattern involved maneuvering by a trailer loaded with calves. They let us introduce our horses to them beforehand, which was great, but Aria had a meltdown trying to take in the calves with other horses swarming around her. She has never been a fan of traffic. During our pattern, she handled the calves much better, and it gave me hope if calves were in the pattern at World. Sure enough, they were. We squeezed in one more lesson with Tracey between hunt seat equitation and ranch riding to work on our pattern. Instead of a pen of calves, we used a fire breathing tractor with flashing lights. The effect was the same, and we worked through it.

At World, Cherie and I stalled next to each other. It was such a joy having our horses together. We show together at club shows, so not only are we friends, but our horses get along well, too. Her horse, affectionately known as Barbie, is much more mellow than Aria at shows, so having him around helped her settle a bit, just like Cherie and I kept each other from getting too nervous. We had been praying for each other through the whole World Show experience, both of us well aware that it was going to take God stepping up and fighting for us for us to do well. My prayer was that if God wanted someone other than me to win, I wanted it to be Cherie. She has always been a source of encouragement for me at shows, and when Momma passed away, she was there for me, encouraging me yet again. I could not ask for a better friend or sister in Christ.

There were originally nine entries in our class, but one scratched during the day. With that many in the class, I knew the only way we would place respectably was if God showed up again. I knew four of the entries. One was Cherie. Her horse is amazing, and they always turn out beautiful rides. One was owned by Sam and

Michelle Reding, the friends who would let me haul to their place and practice in their arena when they lived nearby. Their trainer was riding Sam's horse, Ed, a horse that consistently did well at shows. The third was another trainer Cherie and I show with locally at club shows. She is a sweet lady, and she also always turns out great rides. The fourth was one of my fellow hunt seat equitation riders, a wonderful rider with a good horse, solid on patterns. The rest of the class I did not know, but if they were there, they had to be good. When Cherie and I went to warm up our horses together, we were able to see the other horses, and my suspicion was correct. Everyone looked incredibly talented. My prayers for God to show up continued in earnest. I prayed our performance would give Him glory. I knew the only way we would not be last was if He fought for us once again.

Originally, we were to be fourth to go, but with the scratch, we would be third. Our pattern started off rough. The saddle bags we were to pick up got stuck on the hook, and I had trouble getting them off. Aria repositioned herself, and I got them free. After negotiating the logs, we trotted straight for the pen of calves. Aria's ears shot up, but no spooking or running out. My prayer was that if God can shut the mouths of lions for Daniel in the lions' den, He could shut the mouths of calves for us, and He did! The calves were calm and quiet. Aria was not fazed by them at all. The rest of our pattern went well, not perfect, but solid. We had done our best, and I was thrilled. How we placed would be icing on the cake. We had survived the calves, loped off smartly, got our lead change, had decent pivots, our extended trot was lovely, and our back up was good. She even stood like a saint for me to hang the saddle bags back on the hook. God had blessed. Now we just had to sit and wait and cheer the others on.

After all the patterns were complete, we entered the arena together for placings. I began praying my customary prayer: "please don't let me be last!" It seemed like time stood still as they tallied the scores. Then, one by one they called the placings, starting from the bottom and working their way up. Not me each time. Excitement began to build as I realized I had made the top five!! Fifth place…Still not me! I was shocked with fourth was not me either! Three of us remained: Cherie, Sam and Michelle's horse, and me. I could not fathom beating either of them because their patterns had been spectacular. I was right; I took home third!! I was so proud of Aria!! To go from hunt seat to ranch riding and bring home third in that field was beyond words!! God had shown up again! But it was not over. I rode out of the arena, but I paused outside the gate to hear the final placings. Reserve was announced: Sam's horse! Cherie had done it! She had won World!! God had shown up in a mighty way for both of us! Not only did I come home with third, but my dear friend and fellow amateur laid down a spectacular, nearly flawless pattern, beating out all the professionals, and took home the World Championship!! I was, and am, so thrilled for Cherie, and exceptionally proud of her, too! It could not have happened to a more deserving woman! Both of us faced our fears of showing against professionals, stepped out in faith, and God blessed our obedience and our trust in Him.

We serve and ride for a mighty God. Beyond a shadow of a doubt, the 2017 APHA Open and Amateur World Championship Show is a testament to what happens when He shows up and fights for you. I have likened the whole experience to God parting the Red Sea for the Israelites in Exodus 14. At the time, I had no idea just how accurate that depiction truly was.

Points to Ponder...

- Has there been a time when you were afraid or intimidated by all that you faced when pursuing the dreams God has given you? How did God close those lions' mouths, silencing their roars?

- How has God used fellow believers to encourage you and help you chase your dreams?

- How have you seen God bless them for their willingness to be used by Him?

My Plan **God's Plan**

Promised Land

Promised Land

Jordan River

Red Sea

Wilderness

Red Sea

The Wilderness

"For my thoughts are not your thoughts,
neither are your ways my ways,"
declares the LORD.
"As the heavens are higher than the earth,
so are my ways higher than your ways
and my thoughts than your thoughts."
Isaiah 55:8-9

Chapter 3

The Dream Deferred

"For I know the plans I have for you," declares the LORD,
"plans to prosper you and not to harm you,
plans to give you hope and a future,"
Jeremiah 29:11

My plan after World was to take a couple of weeks off from training and then get right back in the saddle, making use of the platform God had given me through our World Championship. However, this was not God's plan. About a month after World, Aria came up lame. It started off minor, but over the weeks that followed, her healing process was a roller coaster, two steps forward, one step back. One injury would heal, only to be replaced with another. God pushed pause on the dream of Aria and me continuing to point people to Him through our efforts in the show ring. After all the heartache and spiritual warfare we had endured, this was a devastating blow. I thought we had crossed the Red Sea and had finally entered the Promised Land only to discover that we were in the wilderness. I wish I could tell you that in that moment I respectfully told God that I would just use this time to grow and mature in my relationship with Him, which is always the purpose of wilderness experiences in the Bible, but that would not be very truthful. I was angry, hurt, and felt betrayed by God, that He had granted us this incredible blessing of a World Championship only to put us back on a shelf, and at the expense of Aria's soundness as well. God had taken Blue. God had taken Mom. Now God had taken Aria's soundness. I felt punished, for what I did not know, and I did not appreciate Him taking it out on Aria. She had nothing to do with whatever I did, and she did not deserve to be in pain because of me. I felt like Aria and I still had so much to offer God. Surely, the glory He received from World was not all He wanted from us. Surely, He could still use us.

I was doing all I could do for Aria, and it still did not seem to be enough. That was when I felt the Holy Spirit say, "because it is not. It takes Me, too." I realized that my anger and frustration was preventing me from seeing this as another opportunity for God to show His power. God does not just show up to bring victory; He also shows up when we feel defeated to renew our strength and help us persevere. He has a plan to use Aria's injury to bring glory to Himself, just as much as World has, maybe even that the two combined will point even more people to Him than World alone did. My prayers changed from venting my frustration to God to asking for forgiveness. He did not do this to Aria, but He could most definitely use this for good. Wilderness experiences are always times of learning, of refining, so that when we do get to our Promised Land, whatever it is that God has in store for us on the other side of Aria's injury, we appreciate it all the more because we can better see God's hand in every event that led us there, not that He orchestrated every bump in the road, but that He used every bump as a means to intervene and guide us to His best for us rather than the "almost good enough" we were willing to settle for as we approached the wilderness that lay ahead. We do not know what incredible blessings God has in store for us on the other side of what we are going through, but if we let Him lead, if we stick close to Him and listen intently to His voice, He will use the wilderness to refine us into the men and women He wants us to be, who are more capable of serving Him and of appreciating the Promised Land than the person we were going into the wilderness.

Once Israel had crossed the Red Sea and passed through the wilderness, God brought them to the edge of the Promised Land. After listening to the spies' report, the Israelites let their fear overshadow their knowledge of God and His promises, resulting in them wandering in the wilderness for an additional forty years. After God has taken us into the wilderness so that we grow in our relationship with Him and learn more about Him and ourselves, there will come a point when God says it is time to leave the wilderness and follow Him into the Promised Land He has for us, whatever that may be. In that moment, we have a choice: let our fear of the unknown or of the "giants in the land" drown out God's voice and stay in the familiarity of the wilderness, missing out on the blessings God has planned, or put the lessons of the wilderness into action and boldly follow God, trusting Him and His promises. While in the wilderness, it is hard to fathom anyone wanting to stay there instead of moving on into a time of blessing, but all of us take pause when we approach a major life change, even when it is an incredibly beneficial change. Change is difficult and uncomfortable, even when the change is leaving the wilderness for the Promised Land. However, unless we want to wander in the wilderness for a few extra decades that could have been spent enjoying the fulfillment of God's promises, actively serving Him, and pursuing His purpose and calling on our lives, we need to boldly march on when He tells us to, confidently trusting His Word, His grace, and His provision, knowing His presence is always with us.

I do not know what God has in store for us once Aria is healed, but I do know the spiritual lessons learned on this journey are invaluable and are preparing us for whatever Promised Land lies ahead of us. There have been moments of having to step out on faith in order for her recovery to progress, such as leaving support wraps off, gradually increasing turnout space and time turned out, and praying that God protects her and she behaves with her increased freedom. One of the greatest steps of faith came the moment I sat on her for the first time since her injury, riding her at the walk, in an effort to further her rehabilitation, first at the ordinary walk, then pushing her to extend her walk, and then trusting her when she chose to trot a few strides. Tears of joy welled up when she felt normal, despite the fact her leg still looked anything but. There also have been moments where I am utterly unsure of our progress, seeing no difference in the scar tissue, and I have to rely on the difference the vet sees at our weekly laser therapy appointments to know that she truly is improving. All of these moments are steps moving us through this wilderness and inching us towards our Promised Land. In each of these moments, I could have given into the fear and chosen to stay in the comfort of Aria's confinement and limitations, but that would guarantee that she would not heal as well as she could, preventing us from being able to be used by God as well as we could be on the other side of this. It would guarantee we would remain stuck in the wilderness. Each moment has been an opportunity to trust God and trust the vet, and each time it has paid off, just as God promises.

Many of the battles and struggles we face could be called "Red Sea Moments," moments when our back is against the wall, the enemy has us surrounded, and we see no way out. When we begin our journey with God, we are much like the Israelites leaving Egypt. We know we are headed to the Promised Land, but we also whine and complain when the journey gets tough. God allows moments in our journey when we are backed into a corner, hemmed in by the Red Sea on one side and an insurmountable army on the other, as the Israelites were in Exodus 14, a position that is impossible for us to be victorious on our own. This is the position Aria and I were in when we entered the ring at APHA World. We faced stiff competition, tough judges, and battled our own nerves and limitations. This is also the same position we are in battling her injury. These Red Sea Moments give Him the opportunity to step up and fight for us, allowing us and the world to see what happens when God shows up, a victory only He could accomplish. If our journey to the Promised Land God has for us, the fulfillment of the dream He has placed in our hearts, if it were simply a walk in the park, we would not appreciate our dream fulfilled nor would we see His hand in making it come true. Therefore, fulfilling His calling on our lives is much like the Israelites' wilderness experience: difficult, full of moments where God intervenes and shows His hand in events, each time an opportunity for us to learn to trust God in all things and at all times, to learn His character, and to change ours to match. As we journey through the wilderness, God molds and shapes us into His likeness so that we will be wise stewards of our Promised Land and mature enough spiritually to use our Promised Land to bring Him honor and glory and to point others to Him. We realize our calling and our dream fulfilled are only possible because of Him. All our efforts would have been, and are, for naught, if it were not for Him.

These moments are also much like when Jesus asked Peter to step out of the boat and walk to Him on the water. The water swirled around him; the wind howled. As long as Peter's focus was fixed on Jesus, his circumstances, no matter how bleak, did not drag him down. Peter began to sink because he allowed his focus to shift off of Jesus and onto his circumstances. When my focus shifted from God fighting for us and Aria's healing and onto me, my wants, my efforts, my limited perspective of the situation, that is when God began to feel distant, and I began to sink into hurt, anger, and despair. God had not moved. My focus had. The storms of life overwhelm us when our focus is on them and their effects rather than the One calling us to Him. When we get distracted by trying to take care of our circumstances on our own, rather than trusting Jesus to handle them, we start to drown, drown in doubt, self-pity, darkness, hurt, despair, anger. Oswald Chambers in *Our Utmost for His Highest* talks about following God and allowing God to handle the consequences of following Him[4], those storms that pop up and swirl around us when we dare to get out of the boat and walk on water to Jesus. There is great risk stepping out of the boat like Peter did, just like there was great risk when the Israelites struck out for the Promised Land from Egypt. There is even greater risk, though, when we take our eyes off of Jesus. People will not approve when we step out of the boat. People will say we are literally abandoning ship and leaving behind duties, responsibilities, even people. They will say we are foolish and setting ourselves up for trouble. But if God asks us to step out of the boat, He has a plan in place to take care of the boat and all that is in it that we leave behind. He also has a plan to handle the swirling wind, the crashing waves, and the driving rain that surround us when we step out in faith. We need to let Him handle those. We need to just focus on Him, put one foot in front of the other, and keep walking in faith, following His leading, and trusting His calling and direction.

This does not mean, however, that we be oblivious of the storms, of the approaching army, naively ignoring them like an ostrich with its head in the sand, just expecting them to go away. God would not have gotten glory from our performance at World had we not trained and practiced in advance, nor would He if I had not taken Aria to the vet when she came up lame and not followed the vet's treatment instructions. Trusting God to handle life's storms means actively listening to His guidance to see what part He needs us to play in calming the storms or parting the Red Sea. Storms can be diversionary tactics of the enemy designed to distract us from God's will, but they also can be circumstances God allows into our lives to reveal His power and require our involvement to resolve. The Holy Spirit guides us and grants us discernment, storm by storm, moment by moment, as to what God expects of us. All storms should be bathed in prayer; this opens our hearts and minds to the Holy Spirit and the discernment He provides. God also wants us to be honest with Him as to what we want concerning the storms, how we want them to pass or change or what we desire. Multiple times the Gospels recount Jesus knowing people's thoughts and hearts, so He already knows what we want and are thinking. By being honest with Him, ultimately, we are being honest with ourselves. That moment of honesty and clarity allows the Holy Spirit to prick our hearts and show us if our desires line up with God's or not. That is what it took for me to stop blaming God for Aria's injury and start praying for Him to fight for her healing. Sometimes it is not the situation that needs changing, but, rather, we are the ones that need changing, be it aspects of our character that do not align with God's or our perspective needs adjusting to match His. We may not know right away what God's desires are for the situation we face, but our complete honesty will bring us peace, for we have borne all to God.

We naturally pray for God to change difficult situations in our lives. Sometimes He does, and sometimes He does not. We do not always understand why when He does not. All we can do is lean on the truth of Isaiah 55:8-9. His ways are not our ways. His thoughts are not our thoughts. His ways and thoughts are so much greater than ours, it is beyond our comprehension. We just have to trust His reasons and His promises that He will work good from all things, even things meant for evil, as Romans 8:28 and Genesis 50:20 point out. God uses all the trials we face as learning experiences for us. Anytime individuals in the Bible needed to get alone with God to grow, God sent them to the wilderness: the Israelites, John the Baptist, Jesus. The wilderness is tough, harsh. It divides the boys from the men. God does not necessarily send us to the wilderness literally, but He definitely does figuratively through the trials of life. They show us our weaknesses, which is the perfect opportunity for God to show us His strength. In 2 Corinthians 12:9, God promises, "My grace is sufficient for you, for my power is made perfect in weakness." The wilderness, storms, difficult circumstances, are all catalysts for trusting in God's grace, strength, and provision. They are the perfect set up; we just have to learn to let God step up. Wilderness experiences are character building; they either make us bitter or better. The choice is ours. When God does not miraculously change our circumstances, He uses them to change us, to deepen our relationship with Him, to mold us into His image, so we show His grace and reflect Him during our adversity.

We have to cling to the promise of Philippians 1:6. God began a good work in us, and through Christ, He will see it through to completion. God started using Aria and me to point people to Him through what He accomplished through us at World. Yes, He has delayed allowing us to use our World Championship as a platform to share the Gospel and encourage others in their walk with God, but that does not mean that He is finished with us. He started this good work in us. He will see it through in His perfect time. The wilderness, storms, and adversity are all part of the growing process. They are the refiner's fire necessary to get rid of the dross and make us into the men and women God needs us to be, to serve Him as He needs us to serve, and to touch the hearts He needs us to touch. We cannot be the difference in this world until we are different from the world. Without the struggle, we would not see ourselves as the earthen vessels in 2 Corinthians 4:7. God allows our Red Sea Moments, our "get out of the boat" moments, our wilderness experiences so that we see our frailty as well as His power, and they allow us to testify that the only way we do what we do is through Him. Our frailty forms the very cracks that let His power and greatness shine through us.

There is absolutely no way Aria and I could have won a World Championship had God not been fighting for us and going ahead of us. He made that happen. Not us. It will take Him fighting for Aria's healing for her to be 100% restored. The vet and I are doing all we can do, but it will require His mighty, healing power for us to be back in the saddle again. This time in the wilderness has not just been about Aria's healing and growth. It has been a time of healing and growth for me as well. Just like in every wilderness experience described in the Bible, God has been using this time to deepen our relationship and my faith. My prayer is our journey will also encourage you with whatever storm or wilderness you face.

Points to Ponder…

- What wilderness have you found yourself in lately? How did you react to it? What have you learned or are learning from it?

- Has God been asking you to step out of the boat and onto the waves to follow Him? How so? How is God helping you keep your focus on Him rather than the waves?

- How have you seen God work good both in and from your storm? If it is too early to tell, how do you hope He will?

Chapter 4

God's Grace

"as far as the east is from the west,
so far has he removed our transgressions from us."
Psalm 103:12

For many of us, our brokenness causes us to feel unusable by God. Part of my anger about Aria's injury was more fear that God would no longer use us. While her physical brokenness is not the same as spiritual and emotional brokenness, the fear I felt is the same fear we feel when we think we have strayed too far from God. We ask God to forgive our shortcomings, but we cannot seem to forgive ourselves. We have trouble showing ourselves the same grace God shows us, and we have trouble believing that God will still want us to serve Him and represent Him, even after He has forgiven us.

Romans 8:37-39 promises that nothing can separate us from God's love. Nothing we do or do not do can cause us to lose God's love or His grace, or cause Him to love us any less, no matter how broken we think we are. His love and grace are gifts freely given that He will never take back, as Ephesians 2:8-9 testifies. John 10:27-29 says, "My sheep listen to my voice; I know them, and they follow me. I give them eternal life, and they shall never perish; no one can snatch them out of my hand. My Father, who has given them to me, is greater than all; no one can snatch them out of my Father's hand." No one. Not you. Not anyone else. No one can snatch you out of His hand. Once you are His, you are His. Nothing can change that.

When we do not forgive ourselves, or we think some wound we have experienced makes us unusable by God, we inadvertently create distance between us and God. We withdraw from His presence in shame, and it becomes a self-fulfilling prophecy. We think God cannot and will not use us because of our brokenness; however, it is our unwillingness to forgive ourselves, our unwillingness to see ourselves through God's eyes and His grace, not our brokenness, that prevents God from working through us. God can only work through willing, receptive, and obedient hearts. As 2 Corinthians 4:7 testifies, He loves to work through broken, "leaky" vessels because our cracks are what lets His glory and awesomeness seep out for the whole world to see. By closing ourselves off to the possibility of still being usable, we choose to not let God use us. If we do not let Him, then God will respect our wishes and not use us. He will never force us to do anything. That is control and manipulation, not love and grace. As long as I focused on Aria's and my immediate limitations, my heart and mind were closed to the host of ways God can still use us down the road once she heals. He could not give me hope for our future until I let Him. It took time to see that our journey itself is a testimony to God's grace and ability to use us even when we are not perfect, even when we appear broken. It is through our scars that His light shines through. We need to fully comprehend God's grace, just how complete His forgiveness is. We also need to realize that if God Almighty can forgive us, who are we to say what we did is unforgiveable? Who are we to say what someone else did to us is unforgiveable? Are we wiser than God? Are we more just? Most certainly not.

So just how complete is God's grace and forgiveness? Psalm 103:12 tells us that "as far as the east is from the west, so far has he removed our transgressions from us." Picture a globe. If you run your finger north along the surface to the North Pole, once you pass it, your finger is now moving south. Continue moving south, and when you pass the South Pole, your finger is again moving north. North and south meet at the poles. East and west, however, never meet. Run your finger east along the surface, and when you circumference the globe, you are still going east. Same if you go west. When you circumference the globe, you are still moving west. When God removes our transgressions from us, they are completely and entirely gone without a trace. Like east and west never meeting, we never meet our transgressions again. They are forgotten. God chooses to forgive and forget our sin. So important is this fact that it is repeated multiple times in the Bible: Isaiah 43:25, Jeremiah 31:34, Ezekiel 33:16, Hebrews 8:12, Hebrews 10:17. When we ask God to forgive us, He does. Completely. Never to throw it in our face down the road, in this life or the next. He remembers our sin no more. It is gone.

So why do we still feel guilty sometimes even after we ask for God's grace? That is not God. That is us. That is our inability to forgive ourselves. When guilt starts to rear its ugly head, we need to remind ourselves that if God does not hold our mistakes against us, neither should we. 2 Corinthians 5:19-20 tells us that God is committed to our reconciliation to Him, which is why He does not count our mistakes against us when we ask Him for forgiveness. However, if we get hung up in our past, if we cannot let go of our mistakes and forgive ourselves, we are hindering the reconciliation process, and we cannot move forward in our relationship with God. It is like trying to ask a horse to move forward while sitting in the saddle backwards. You are not going to get very far that way. At the very least, you will not get to where you intended. We have to forgive ourselves, let go of the past, learn from it, and then turn around in the saddle and let Jesus take the reins. Only then can our relationship truly be right with God, the kind of relationship He intends for us to have. We need to give Him our lives completely in return for His Son's life, letting Him lead in all areas of our lives. We have to let Him have the reins of our lives and steer us down the path He has planned for us. He will never snatch the reins from our hands. When we give Him our lives, we can then enjoy His presence and the peace and comfort He brings. No guilt. No shame. Just acceptance, love, and grace. Being in His presence, we develop a deep desire on our part to please Him in all that we say and do, modifying our behavior to reflect Him and share about His grace to others so that they too can enjoy His presence.

Again, you can only enter into and enjoy God's presence and its benefits if you have given Jesus the reins of your life and accepted His gift of grace and forgiveness. It is imperative that you get that part right between you and God before we go any further down this trail. In John 14:6, "Jesus answered, 'I am the way and the truth and the life. No one comes to the Father except through me.'" "[F]or all have sinned and fall short of the glory of God, and are justified freely by his grace through the redemption that came by Christ Jesus. God presented him as a sacrifice of atonement through faith in his blood. He did this to demonstrate his justice, because in his forbearance he had left the sins committed beforehand unpunished." Romans 3:23-25. "For the wages of sin is death, but the gift of God is eternal life in Christ Jesus our Lord." Romans 6:23. "For God so loved the world that he gave his one and only Son, that whoever believes in him shall not perish but have eternal life." John 3:16. "That if you confess with your mouth, 'Jesus is Lord,' and believe in your heart that God raised him from the dead, you will be saved." Romans 10:9. "For it is by grace you have been saved, through faith — and this not from ourselves, it is the gift of God — not by works, so that no one can boast." Ephesians 2:8-9. Giving your life to Christ is simple, so simple, in fact, that children understand it, and adults try to complicate it.

It starts with admitting that you are not perfect, that you have disobeyed God, damaging your relationship with Him, and you cannot fix your relationship with God on your own, not by your own merit or by working hard enough. An imperfect person cannot enter the presence of a perfect God. It would be like trying to pour a glass of dirty water into a pitcher of clean water expecting the pitcher to remain pure and clean. It all becomes dirty. While we can filter water and make it pure again, if God tried to filter out all our impurities, there would be nothing left because our disobedient nature is entwined with every fiber of our being. Deuteronomy 4:24 says, "For the LORD your God is a consuming fire, a jealous God." He is jealous for us and wishes to burn off all the impurities, the sin, the rebelliousness, the disobedience, the dross, that prevent us from entering His presence. However, if He tried to burn off all the dross from our lives, again, we would be completely consumed by the fire; nothing would remain to enter God's presence. That is why the wages of sin is death and why God left our sins unpunished before Christ entered the picture. We would die unable to be in His presence, thus eternally separated from God. God loves us, He loves YOU, too much to let that happen. He created us, He created YOU, to be in His presence, not to be separated from Him. So, He sent His perfect Son to earth, to endure betrayal, shame, torture, crucifixion, an excruciatingly horrible and gruesome death, to take all our sin, all our disobedience, rebellion, and imperfections, upon Himself. He died in our place, allowing Himself to be separated from God so that we would never have to endure that separation.

You may know all these facts, but I want you to let them sink into your heart. Do you realize that if you were the only person in all of history that ever disobeyed God or ever would disobey God, if you were the only person who would ever be separated from God, God would still have sent Jesus, and Jesus would still have endured all of it? Just. For. YOU. He wants a relationship with YOU that much. He loves YOU that much. YOU are that precious, that treasured, that important. Jesus died for YOU.

Because of Jesus's obedience to God, when He died, God rewarded Him with new life. When Jesus died in our sin, our sin separated Him from God. In order for Jesus to enter God's presence again, God had to remove our sin, our death, from Him and replace it with new, perfect, resurrected life, fully restored, fully righteous. Jesus's perfect obedience to God allowed God to do this. It allowed God to remove our unrighteousness that Jesus had taken on to Himself and replace it with God's perfect righteousness, the same righteousness Jesus offers us in exchange for our unrighteousness, if we are willing to give it to Him. The Resurrection proves to all who will listen with an open mind and an open heart that Jesus truly is the Son of God. No other man could have lived in perfect obedience to God.

Since our sin, our disobedience, our unrighteousness has been removed, and Jesus's righteousness has been credited to us, God looks at us through the lens of Jesus's righteousness, seeing us as perfect, having a restored relationship with Him, and we can be in His presence. That is, of course, IF we give Him our life in return for the life Jesus gave us. It is not a trade if both parties do not exchange something of value. Jesus cannot trade us His life, His righteousness for our life, our unrighteousness, if we do not authorize the exchange. We have to accept the gift of grace offered to us: the pardon made available to us through Jesus, His righteousness, His perfect life that He offered up for us. In return, we give Him our brokenness, our unrighteousness, our sins, our failings, our disobedience in return. We need to let Him take them from us, ask Him to forgive us, and accept His grace, His righteousness, and His new life in return. We give up control of our lives, give Him the reins, and let Him guide us as to how to live, how to act, how to be more and more like Him each day, not out of obligation, but out of gratitude for what He has done for us.

If you have not done this, will you do this right now? Will you ask Him to forgive you? Will you thank Him for His grace? Will you give Him your life in exchange for His? Will you ask Him to take charge of your life from here on out? If you do, it is the best decision you will ever make, one with both earthly and eternal blessings. Your eternity in God's presence starts the second you accept His gift of grace. It starts here on earth in this life and continues on into the next.

Points to Ponder...

- Take a moment to really let all of this soak in: God's grace. Jesus's sacrifice. God's love for you. Let it filter down from just knowing these facts to letting them take root in your heart.

- Have you given Jesus the reins of your life? If so, how has it made a difference? If not, what is stopping you?

- What brokenness are you allowing to come between you and God? What can you do to make a conscious effort to forgive yourself and stop holding it against yourself?

Chapter 5

God's Presence

"…And surely I am with you always, to the very end of the age."
Matthew 28:20b

This new life we now have allows us unfettered access to God's presence and all its benefits. All He asks in return is our love, devotion, and gratitude. Out of this comes a desire to live in a manner pleasing to Him. We will still fall short, still stumble, still disobey from time to time, but no matter what we do, He will still forgive us and love us and see us as His adopted children. He will never cast us out of His presence. "The LORD replied, 'My Presence will go with you, and I will give you rest.'" Exodus 33:14. No matter where we go, God's presence will be with us, strengthening us, comforting us, renewing our soul.

When the Israelites left Egypt, Exodus 13:21-22 tells us that God went ahead of them. His presence was a visible pillar of fire at night and of cloud by day. How incredible it must have been to actually see that God was with them and was leading them. There would have been no reason to doubt where to go. Just literally follow God. Even though we cannot see God's presence like the Israelites could, He still goes ahead of us, blazing a trail. Deuteronomy 31:8 says, "The LORD himself goes before you and will be with you; he will never leave you nor forsake you. Do not be afraid; do not be discouraged." Think on this. There is great comfort in this verse. God goes before us. No matter what lies ahead of us, God is already there making a way for us with a plan to use whatever we face for our good. We will never face anything that God does not already have a plan to handle. But God does not just go before us. He also is with us, walking along side us, holding us, guiding us, comforting us, and with God at our side, we have no reason to fear or be discouraged. His presence will carry us through, both good times and difficult times.

The King James Version adds another layer of hope. Momma would always quote this version of her favorite verse. "And the LORD, he it is that doth go before thee; he will be with thee, he will not fail thee, neither forsake thee: fear not, neither be dismayed." Not only will God not leave us, but He will not fail us. He will never let us down. Even when life seems overwhelming and incredibly difficult, He will see us through. Not only do we not need to fear, there is no need to be distraught because He is with us, leading the way. There is comfort in His presence. When Momma went into the hospital that last time, none of us knew, herself included, that she would not come home. However, God went before us, preparing all of our hearts, and He was with us when she did pass, filling us with peace and comfort that we would see her again. The days and months since have not been easy, with some being rather dark, but God's abiding presence has kept us from being overwhelmed with grief. This same abiding peace was with us when we went to World. God's presence went ahead of us and filled the arena. He was with us every footfall of our patterns, every moment of our rail work, and He was at our side as the placings were announced. When tears of joy mixed with grief rained down, He caught every one of them and wrapped His comforting arms around both Daddy and me, allowing us to not only feel His presence, but Momma's as well.

Psalm 23 is one of the most recognized passages in the Bible, and it paints a beautiful picture of God's comforting presence. When we are in the green pastures of life, God's presence encourages us to take time to rest and be restored. When times are good, we can get caught up in doing, in serving, in enjoying life, which is what we should do, like a sheep enjoying lush, green grass, but if we fail to take quiet moments to reflect and renew, we will burn out. We pour our hearts out in service, but without rest to refill the cup of our spirit, it will run empty. You cannot pour from an empty cup. God knows this, so His presence encourages us to know when to rest and when to move on down the path of righteousness, the path of living as God wants us to live. When our path enters dark time of grief, loss, or heartache, His presence gives us hope. This Psalm gives us hope. The psalmist said, "though I walk THROUGH the valley of the shadow of death" (emphasis mine). Through. Not parked in. Not camped out in. Not bogged down and stuck in. Through. We go THROUGH the valleys. God's presence makes valleys temporary. How? Because the Good Shepherd is leading us. His rod and staff, His guidance and His presence, comfort us. When life seems dark, though the shadow of the valley dims the light of joy, if we keep listening to His voice, keep following His leading, keep leaning into His ever faithful, comforting arms, we will get through the valley to the brighter days the psalmist describes, days of feasting, of the cup of our spirit being refilled to overflowing, of goodness and love, all because we chose to dwell in God's presence. His presence will see Aria and me through this dark time. It is not our final destination. Better days lie ahead for us, just as this Psalm promises.

Jesus draws upon this illustration in John 10. How beautiful are verses 14 and 15: "I am the good shepherd; I know my sheep and my sheep know me — just as the Father knows me and I know the Father — and I lay down my life for the sheep." God knows us. Jesus knows us. Not in the sense of just being aware we exist, but in the sense of loving us, cherishing us, knowing every detail about us. In Genesis 16:13, Hagar calls God "the One who sees me." It is a horrible feeling to feel invisible. Sadly, many of us know that feeling all too well. Be in a group, and no one seems to notice us or even care to attempt to include us. We are unseen. Invisible. An outsider. An outlier. God sees us, though. We are His sheep that He calls by name. We are His sheep that He laid down His life for. John 15:13 says there is no greater love than to lay down your life for your friend. In this same chapter, Jesus calls us His friends. Wrap your mind around that for a second. You. Me. Jesus's friends. The God who made the entire universe, the King of kings, the Lord of lords, the Great I Am...calls us His friend. We may doubt our value to others, but there is absolutely no doubt as to our value to God. We are His friends. Chosen. Treasured. Loved. Priceless. To die for. Our value does not come from our relationship with other people, or lack thereof. Our value comes from our relationship with God.

There is no greater honor than to be considered God's friend and His child, as John 1:12 describes us. "Yet to all who receive him, to those who believed in his name, he gave the right to become children of God." We become His children when we receive God's grace through Jesus, but becoming His friend requires effort on our part. The only way you become friends with someone is to spend time in each other's presence and truly get to know each other. God knows everything about us, our likes, dislikes, talents, insecurities, dreams, every spot, wrinkle, and tan line, and guess what? He loves us no matter what. "How great is the love the Father has lavished on us, that we should be called children of God! And that is what we are!" 1 John 3:1a&b. To Him, we are never invisible, never an outlier, never an outsider. We are sheep in His fold. Loved. Protected. Comforted. Treasured. Chosen. He sees us. But friendship must be reciprocated for it to be real. God knows everything about us, but we need to spend time in His presence to get to know Him, to fully understand who He is and what He stands for. We must spend time in His Word, praying, listening to the Holy Spirit, for our friendship with God to truly blossom and flourish. Aria and I would not have the bond that we have and the ability to perform together like we do if we did not spend time together. Over the years we have learned each other's personalities, quirks, talents, and even limits. We have earned each other's love, respect, and trust. We see each other. That is something that takes time and effort, just like building a strong relationship with God does.

Sometimes, though, we get so busy that, while God sees us, we do not see Him. Jeremiah 29:12-13 says, "Then you will call upon me and come and pray to me, and I will listen to you. You will seek me and find me when you seek me with all your heart." God promises to hear us when we call out to Him, for guidance, wisdom, our needs, our wants, but we have to put Him first, ahead of all of the busyness. Only then will we find Him and truly see Him and His will. Psalm 46:10a tells us to "Be still and know that I am God." Be still. The frantic pace of life can make it incredibly hard to stop and be still, for any reason at all. It is imperative, though, that we take time to be still in God's presence and wait on Him. Isaiah 40:31 (KJV) reminds us that "they that wait upon the LORD shall renew their strength; they shall mount up with wings like eagles; they shall run, and not be weary; they shall walk, and not faint." I can still hear Momma sing this verse in song, which goes on to say, "teach me, Lord, teach me, Lord, to wait." Waiting in God's presence, being still before Him, gives Him the chance to speak to us, to renew our spirit, to refill our cup that gets poured out in service to Him and to others. It is a chance for Him to strengthen us and encourage us. Aria's injury has forced me to be still before God and wait on Him to move, wait on Him to heal her. This stillness has given Him the opportunity to heal my wounds as well, restoring my heart and deepening my relationship with Him. This time is also allowing Him to shine a light in my heart and clarify His calling for my life. I would not have taken this sabbatical had it not been for her injury. I would have pressed on, focused on the big picture of God's plan for us, forging ahead into territory that God knew we were not ready to possess yet. Just like the Israelites needed the time in the wilderness to prepare their hearts for the Promised Land, God knew I needed time to prepare my heart for whatever it is He has in store for us once Aria heals.

Isaiah 41:10 goes on to say that God will strengthen us and help us, holding us up with His righteous hand. Being still before God gives us a leg up back into the saddle when life has bucked us off. His presence is a place of peace, comfort, renewal, restoration, and strengthening. It is where God reminds us that He is for us, and as Paul said in Romans 8:31, "If God is for us, who can be against us?" God is our greatest ally in life "…because the one who is in you is greater than the one who is in the world." 1 John 4:4b. God's presence in you is greater than any foe, earthly or spiritual, that you will ever face. God's presence will never leave you, just as He promised in Deuteronomy 31:8. He is faithful to keep His promises. "For great is your love, reaching to the heavens; your faithfulness reaches to the skies." Psalm 57:10. Great is His faithfulness.

"Because of the LORD's great love we are not consumed, for his compassions never fail. They are new every morning; great is your faithfulness. I say to myself, 'The LORD is my portion; therefore I will wait for him.' The LORD is good to those whose hope is in him, to the one who seeks him; it is good to wait quietly for the salvation of the LORD." Lamentations 3:22-26. God desires to be our portion and strength. His love and compassion for us can never be tapped out, for they are "new every morning." He longs for us to come to Him and enjoy His presence. He shows kindness to those who trust in Him and wait for Him, His guidance, and provision. As the hymn says, "Great is Thy faithfulness! Morning by morning new mercies I see; All I have needed Thy hand hath provided; Great is Thy faithfulness, Lord, unto me!"[5] God will always be faithful to us. All He asks is that we be faithful to Him in return.

Points to Ponder...

- What are some ways you can be still before the Lord to enjoy His presence?

- How has God refilled your cup and renewed your strength when you have needed it most?

- How does it encourage you, knowing that you are truly seen by God and fully accepted?

Chapter 6

Preparation

"Study to show thyself approved unto God,
a workman that needeth not to be ashamed,
rightly dividing the word of truth."
2 Timothy 2:15 (KJV)

Once we know we have access to God's presence, we then have to actually take advantage of this privilege. Knowing you can call someone is entirely different from actually picking up the phone and dialing. God's presence is always around us, but we have to learn to recognize it. We have to learn His character, His ways, in order to discern His voice from all the others. Charles Spurgeon once said, "Discernment is not a matter of simply telling the difference between right and wrong; rather it is the difference between right and almost right."[6] So much "almost right" is done under the guise of God's name, when God is NEVER almost right. He is ALWAYS right. The key discerning between the two is spending time in God's presence, in God's Word, so much so that walking with Him is as natural as breathing and anything out of step with Him stands out glaringly. Aria and I have to spend time together to learn when we are right versus almost right. The only way I knew she was injured was because I knew how she normally feels when I ride, how she normally looks and moves, when she is "right" so that when she is off or "almost right" I can quickly tell.

Being able to recognize this quickly can be the difference between an injury that heals with time and permanent unsoundness. Being able to recognize "right" from "almost right" in our behavior, in our choices, in the teachings we hear, and well as in the actions of others, can likewise be the difference between maintaining a right relationship with God, having a momentary stumble in our walk, or tumbling down a shady path of darkness we mistook for light.

The time Aria and I spend together not only helps me distinguish when she is off, but it also helps me know when she is spot on. If I had worked with her just once a week, for maybe an hour, leading up to World, our performance would have greatly suffered. Earning our World Championship was no easy task or small feat. It took riding, practicing, and training five to six days a week in order for us to hone our skills and polish our performance, becoming stronger, wiser, and better able to withstand the pressure of competition. It also took working with professional trainers who would give their input and perspective from their years of experience, as well as applying those lessons in our daily practice. It required hours in the saddle to improve and for the new skills we learned during our lessons to become habits.

This goes for our walk with Christ as well. We cannot expect to withstand all that life throws at us or know how God wants us to live and handle situations in a Godly manner when we only spend an hour with God at church on Sundays. Yes, we need those lessons with a "professional," a preacher, a small group leader, or a spiritual mentor that, while they themselves are still not perfect, they are rooted deeper in God's Word than we are and are thus more spiritually mature and able to give us guidance, clarity, and discernment we would otherwise not have, much like a trainer sharing from their experience. However, it takes much more than that. We have to put into practice daily what we learn in our time at church and Bible studies. We have to spend those hours in the saddle, so to speak, delving into God's Word, falling on our knees before Him, seeking His face and His guidance in all we do and face, so that we can apply those lessons to our lives and become more and more like Christ.

2 Timothy 2:15 (KJV) puts it well: "Study to show thyself approved unto God, a workman that needeth not to be ashamed, rightly dividing the word of truth." The only way to correctly understand God and His Word and live in a way that He approves, is to study. Study passages in context of the culture in which it was written and the culture to whom it was directed. Analyze God's behavior towards individuals in the Bible in relation to what the Bible reveals about His character. Look past the surface of God's directives to discover the why behind them, further profiling His character and gaining a deeper understanding and appreciation for His concern for us. Knowing God's character and His expectations for us helps us see when His hand is in a situation and when it is not. "Whether you turn to the right or to the left, your ears will hear a voice behind you, saying, "This is the way; walk in it." Isaiah 30:21. No matter what we are going though, what decisions we face, God will tell us

which path to take and which to avoid. The only way we can recognize Jesus's voice in our life as He describes in John 10 is to study His voice in the Written Word. We have to know what Jesus's voice sounds like before we can recognize it.

God gives us the sound of His voice in 1 Kings 19:11-13. "The LORD said, 'Go out and stand on the mountain in the presence of the LORD, for the LORD is about to pass by.' Then a great and powerful wind tore the mountains apart and shattered the rocks before the LORD, but the LORD was not in the wind. After the wind there was an earthquake, but the LORD was not in the earthquake. After the earthquake came a fire, but the LORD was not in the fire. After the fire came a gentle whisper. When Elijah heard it, he pulled his cloak over his face and went out and stood at the mouth of the cave. Then a voice said to him, 'What are you doing here, Elijah?'" God's voice is not booming, intimidating, or overpowering like a strong wind or earthquake or fire. It is a gentle whisper, or as the KJV says, "a still small voice." His voice is a nudge, not a shove. It is those thoughts that pop into our minds that are not even fully formed, just a quiet image or idea that inspires us and then begins to blossom. Concepts that seem to keep popping up in unrelated places or sources. Recurring themes. This gentle, small voice gives us ideas we would have never thought of on our own. The moment they pop into our minds, it is as if a light bulb comes on, and we gasp and exclaim, "That's it!" As this new-found solution or understanding takes root and blossoms, we are filled with peace and wonder as we realize we just heard the voice of God. If an idea, gut feeling, or suggestion in our life lines up with what we know to be true based on God's Word, then odds are we are recognizing God's voice. It has to line up with God's Word as a whole, however, not just one verse out of context. When Satan tempted Jesus in the wilderness in Luke 4, he used scripture out of context to try to trip Jesus up. If Satan used that tactic on Jesus, the Son of God, he will most certainly use it on us fallible humans. Therefore, it is imperative that we be grounded in God's Word and tapped into God's presence. Then we are able to see God's right and Satan's almost right.

Everything we say and do needs to be bathed in prayer. Prayer is stepping into God's presence and having a conversation with our Friend. We present our praises, our concerns, and our petitions, but we also listen for what God is trying to say to us. John 16:12-15 tells us that Jesus has so much more to say to us than what we can handle at one time. The Holy Spirit's job is to reveal to us what we need to know moment by moment, about God, His Word, His character, even about ourselves, based on and within the context of the Bible. In John 14:26, Jesus says, "But the Counselor, the Holy Spirit, whom the Father will send in my name, will teach you all things and will remind you of everything I have said to you." There are so many issues that are not covered in God's Word. Nowhere does it discuss social media or gun control or which mortgage company to use. It does, however, give us a framework of God's character and His expectations for how we should behave and make decisions that the Holy Spirit will draw upon and point out to us when we seek God's face and His guidance for these and any other issue not specifically spelled out in the Bible, as well as those issues on which Jesus specifically taught.

"To the Jews who had believed him, Jesus said, 'If you hold to my teachings, you really are my disciples. Then you will know the truth and the truth will set you free.'" John 8:31-32. Spending time before God in prayer and in His Word gives us the ability to discern truth from half-truth, for we know His truth and THE Truth, Jesus. Both His truth and The Truth will set us free, free from the bondage of sin, free from fear, free from doubt, free from lies. This does not mean that we will always instantly know what path to take when making a decision, that we will never slip up and sin or doubt or fear, or never fall for Satan's lies. It means that we are not bound and trapped by any of these anymore. We are no longer stuck in any of these patterns of behavior. When we are tempted to act as we once did or we stumble back into old ways, God's truth will shine a light on the situation we find ourselves in and show us a way out, be it by giving us clarity or peace or a reminder of who He is and who we are to Him. 1 Corinthians 10:13 reminds us that when Satan comes knocking with his lies and temptations, God will not let him push us past our limits. He will provide a way out, a way to defeat him.

Hearing God's voice in that moment requires ample preparation beforehand. Proverbs 21:31 says, "The horse is made ready for the day of battle, but victory rests with the LORD." When training a horse for show, or for war, as this verse references, you instill in them all the skills and abilities that could possibly be required of them. You do your best to expect the unexpected and prepare for anything and everything. Victory, however, is not in your hands or in the horse's hooves. It rests on if God shows up and blesses your efforts. If your heart and motives are right with Him, and your intention is to bring Him glory, win or lose, He will show up in a mighty way, just like He did for us at World. That is why this verse is on Aria's stall sign that we hang on her door at shows. It is a constant reminder, to ourselves and to everyone who walks by, Who gets the credit and the glory. We do our part. He does His. When we battle temptation or trials, all our time training in God's presence is put to the test, just like a horse at a show or at war, but God will grant us victory if we listen to His voice, a voice we know well from spending time with Him.

Paul is referring to this quality time with God in Romans 12:2 when he says, "Do not conform any longer to the pattern of this world, but be transformed by the renewing of your mind. Then you will be able to test and approve what God's will is — his good, pleasing and perfect will." Our mind is renewed and transformed in God's presence by His Word and through prayer. We conform to His will rather than our own or that of the world. As we are transformed, we learn to not trust our own judgement, but to trust His. Then we are able to "Trust in the LORD with all your heart and lean not on your own understanding; in all your ways acknowledge him, and he will make your paths straight." Proverbs 3:5-6. Being in His presence transforms us so that we can clearly see His guidance and the path He has laid out for us. We may only see just one step of that path clearly, but we know to trust Him to reveal the next step when we are ready for it.

God's transforming presence not only teaches us to trust His judgement, it changes our hearts so that our desires realign to match His. "Delight yourself in the LORD and he will give you the desires of your heart." Psalm 37:4. When we delight in God, we want what He wants, knowing that will be what is best for us and will bring Him the most honor and glory. Our desire becomes that His will is done in our lives, and that God will most definitely grant. He has no issue giving us any desire that lines up with His will. That does not mean, though, that God will always grant us the desires of our heart the instant we ask. It does mean, however, that when the time is right, when it will be of the greatest benefit to us and to God's purpose for us, when it will bring Him the most honor and glory, God will make it happen and provide. This time between asking and receiving can turn into a wilderness experience, a time of growth and testing, and a time of God's provision in Red Sea Moments. This gives us a better appreciation, though, for what He provides simply because of all we went through for God to grant it to us. This time also transforms us and gives us a better perspective on who we are to God and who He needs us to be to fulfill His purpose and plan.

Points to Ponder…

- Do you currently spend time daily in God's Word, either through reading the Bible Itself or through the guidance of a devotional? If so, how have you seen God speak through it? If not, what are some ways you can start setting aside some time for God?

- Think of a time when you found yourself facing an "almost right" situation. How did you recognize it? If you did not at first, how did God show you to get out of the situation later?

- How has being in God's presence and listening to His voice shaped your desires and plans? Have you felt Him shift your focus as you grow in your walk with Him? How so?

Chapter 7

God's Perspective of Us

"Before I formed you in the womb I knew you,
before you were born I set you apart;
I appointed you as a prophet to the nations."
Jeremiah 1:5

Until we clearly see who we are in Christ, we cannot clearly see
what He has called us to do. So many of us struggle with our worth
and our identity, myself included, even though we know our value
comes from our relationship with God, and we know just how
much He loves us. Sometimes we just need further affirmation to
silence the doubts and lies about ourselves that we are so tempted
to believe. "For we are God's workmanship, created in Christ Jesus
to do good works, which God prepared in advance for us to do."
Ephesians 2:10. This means we are God's masterpiece. Every
aspect of us, our character, our talents, our physical traits, all of it
uniquely woven together for a purpose. Every aspect of who we
are equips us to be used by God for a purpose uniquely our own, as
individualized as we are. We are "fearfully and wonderfully made;
your works are wonderful, I know that full well." Psalm 139:14.
When God created each of us, He saw us as "good," just as He saw
everything in the beginning during Creation. Just like when an
artist finishes a project, steps back to admire their work, and smiles
at the results, when God made you, He stepped back and smiled,

pleased with His masterpiece. Every detail about us was carefully considered and planned, from our eye color to our hair color to our skin tone to precisely how tall we will be, even the unique design of our fingerprints. None of it was by chance. God personally picked out each and every one of your traits. You are that special to Him, that important, and just like any artist, He takes pride in you, for you are a masterpiece.

Psalm 139:13 says, "For you created my inmost being, you knit me together in my mother's womb." That is a beautiful illustration of how intricately God designed us. Knitting is done one stitch at a time following a pattern for an item with a specific purpose. The purpose is picked first, then the pattern is chosen to best suit the purpose of the item, and next the knitting commences. Isaiah 49:1 and Jeremiah 1:5 both say the Lord calls us before we are born. He decides our purpose and then designs us intricately with all that we need to fulfill His purpose for us. Knowing how much thought and care God put into creating each of us should affirm our worth and identity in Him. We are His. Designed by God. Unique. Chosen for a purpose. Saved by grace. Restored through Jesus. When lies and doubts come knocking, use those truths to send them running.

As pointed out in Hebrews 13:21, God will equip us with everything good needed to fulfill His will for our lives. This does not mean that we are born fully equipped to serve God. Otherwise newborns would be as articulate as Paul or Billy Graham at professing the Gospel. This means that we are born with the potential and natural talents we need, and God will orchestrate opportunities in our lives to grow and develop the traits and skills our purpose requires, as well as bring the right people into our lives to mentor us and encourage us to be the men and women God needs us to be to do what He needs us to do.

God's design when He knitted us together was not just for our biological make-up. It extends to our entire being and maps out our entire life. "Every good and perfect gift is from above, coming down from the Father of heavenly lights, who does not change like shifting shadows." James 1:17. Every gift and talent is granted to us by God and clues us into our calling and purpose. If He gives us the ability, He expects us to use it to bring Him glory. That was the reason behind granting us the gift in the first place. This does not happen all at once though. It takes time for our talents, skills, and gifts to develop. Fulfilling our purpose happens in stages. It grows as we grow. As our talents and gifts develop and we mature in Him and in our abilities, He expands how He wants us to use our gifts and gives us different platforms upon which to serve Him. Much like as Aria and I became more proficient, we progressed from local open shows to regional breed shows and then on to APHA World. We would only move up when we were ready and could handle the tougher competition. Much like in the Parable of the Talents, Matthew 25:14-30, and of the Ten Minas, Luke 19:11-27, as we show God we can be responsible over a little, using our talents and gifts effectively, then He will increase our territory, granting us more responsibility in our service to Him, such as going from attending a Bible study to filling in occasionally for the study's leader to leading the study on a regular basis. As we grow, God's purpose for us matches our level of spiritual maturity.

In the meantime, "Don't let anyone look down on you because you are young, but set an example for the believers in speech, in life, in love, in faith and in purity." 1 Timothy 4:12. No matter our stage in life – young, old, or in between – or our stage in our walk with Christ – still wet behind the ears with baptismal waters or seasoned followers wisened with years of close fellowship with Christ – we are to do our best to reflect Christ in all we say and do, being an example that inspires other believers at any stage of life to do likewise. Our age is irrelevant to God. He knows how many years He has given us and expects us to make the most of them. He simply shows us how His purpose for us takes different forms at different seasons of life. So, young or old, never feel like you cannot be used by God. That is just another one of the enemy's lies trying to make you question your worth.

We may feel inadequate at times, but God's advice to us is the same as what He gave to Samuel. "The LORD does not look at the things man looks at. Man looks at the outward appearance, but the LORD looks at the heart." 1 Samuel 16:7b. To the world, we may not measure up to their expectations, but God knows what we are made of because He was the one who knitted us together. He sees our heart and knows who we are and knows what we are truly capable of. We are enough because of Him. His purpose for you lines up perfectly with your character, your talents, your personality, your passions. It will stretch you and encourage you to grow, but it fits you perfectly. We are not perfect, and we are going to mess up, but that is exactly why God wants to use us. "But we have this treasure in jars of clay to show that this all-surpassing power is from God and not from us." 2 Corinthians 4:7. God wants to use broken, leaky people so that we let His light shine through. If we could accomplish His will, His purpose, on our own, people would give us the credit. That is why God gives us a purpose greater than ourselves. When people see us accomplish something that we in no way could do on our own merit, then they know God had to be involved, and He gets the credit He is due. Aria and I absolutely could not have won a World Championship without God's help. We were the leaky vessels that He chose to let His power and light shine through, and our Cinderella story continues to bear witness to Him and His might. The same is true for this road to recovery Aria is on. God is somehow going to get more glory through this than if this had not happened. If she emerges unscarred, it will testify to His miraculous healing power and how through His grace, He will take our brokenness and restore us completely, making us perfectly whole and perfectly usable by Him, her physical healing equating to our spiritual healing. If she is scarred by her injury, then it will testify to how God can and will still use us even with all our scars and imperfections. Only time will tell how He will receive glory through all this.

God uses the ordinary to accomplish the extraordinary because He is the extra that makes all the difference and brings it about. He chooses us. He chooses YOU. He will never reject us. He will never reject YOU. In Isaiah 41:9-10, God says, "I took you from the ends of the earth, from its farthest corners I called you. I said, 'You are my servant'; I have chosen you and have not rejected you. So do not fear, for I am with you; do not be dismayed for I am your God. I will strengthen you and help you; I will uphold you with my righteous right hand." No matter how far we feel from God or how far we have strayed, because of the grace afforded to us by Jesus, God will call us back to Himself, strengthening us, helping us, sustaining us to follow Him, His leading, and pursue His purpose for us. In John 15:13-17, Jesus takes our relationship with Him one step further. He says He no longer calls us servants, but friends, friends hand-picked by God to bear lasting fruit, to make a lasting impact on our world. Because of grace, we are no longer mere servants blindly following orders in obedience to our Master. We are now friends of Christ, friends of God, part of the inner circle that not only knows what is expected of them, but also why. We are loved. We are cherished. We are trusted. We are respected.

Think on this. You and I are friends with Jesus, with God. Real friends can be in short supply in this world. People come and go in our lives, here for the good times and then walk away when the path gets rocky. But we have "a friend who sticks closer than a brother." Proverbs 18:24b. Jesus will never walk away from us, no matter what. We are too precious to Him, YOU are too precious to

Him, for Him to ever allow you to go through life alone. He will be with us, the Holy Spirit will be within us, and He will put the right people into our lives and remove the wrong people, so that our friendship with Him will flourish and our relationships with others will be built on a common bond with Him.

In Matthew 21:42, Jesus says, "The stone the builders rejected has become the capstone; the Lord has done this, and it is marvelous in our eyes." The world may reject us because we do not fit the mold they try to stuff us in, but God has made us an integral part of His plan, the capstone that holds the whole overreaching arch together. There is no more marvelous of a feeling than to truly grasp just how precious and important you are to God. "But you are a chosen people, a royal priesthood, a holy nation, a people belonging to God, that you may declare the praise of Him who called you out of darkness into His wonderful light." 1 Peter 2:9. Chosen. Royal. Holy. Belonging to God. This is you. This is me. We have every reason to praise God because of this. He called us out of darkness and made us new. "Therefore, if anyone is in Christ, he is a new creation; the old has gone, the new has come!" 2 Corinthians 5:17. He has given us a new heart and a new spirit. He has removed our heart of stone and given us a tender heart receptive to Him, His Word, His leading, His spirit, as Ezekiel 36:26 says.

We will still have times when we stumble and times of doubt, and in those times God will still be there and hear us when we, like the psalmist, ask Him to "Create in me a pure heart, O God, and renew a steadfast spirit within me." Psalm 51:10. He will wipe our slate clean again and give us a fresh start. Every single time. God is clear in what He expects of us as His chosen people. "He has shown you, O mortal, what is good. And what does the LORD require of you? To act justly and to love mercy and to walk humbly with your God." Micah 6:8 (NIV 2011). This is litmus our behavior should pass, and there is no greater example to glean from than the life of Christ Himself. He is the role model we all should try to emulate. Even though we will fall short of His perfection, we should strive to be more and more like Him every day.

The key to remember is we are to be like Christ – not like every other believer. God did not make cookie cutter children. He made unique individuals, so we need to strive to be the most Christ-like version of ourselves, rather than a carbon copy or clone of some other believer. All those traits that make you distinctly you, do not lose them unless they are traits you know are not pleasing to God. In all actuality, the closer to God you get, the more truly YOU you become. All that dross we mentioned before will slowly melt away, leaving only the YOU God created you to be, the YOU He has seen you as all along.

Points to Ponder...

- How does knowing God purposefully and carefully planned each detail about you affect how you see yourself?

- What descriptor of how God sees us speaks most to your heart? Why?

- How can knowing how God sees you help you when you are dealing with rejection or mistreatment by others or when you feel alone in a crowd?

Chapter 8

Purpose

*"But we have this treasure in jars of clay to show
that this all-surpassing power is from God and not from us."*
2 Corinthians 4:7

Once we start seeing ourselves as God sees us, we begin to see how
God orchestrates events and circumstances in our lives to guide us
to His purpose for us and to better equip us to fulfill His role for us.
Spending time in His presence and in His Word grants us
discernment as to what that entails and how He will use what He
allows to happen in our lives to further His plans. Understanding
our purpose changes our perspective on our circumstances as well
as gives us insight into God's provision and protection as we
pursue His purpose for His lives. Knowing God's purpose for Aria
and me is to bring Him glory and to point people to Him changes
my perspective on our current wilderness experience of her injury.
It gives me hope that this is not the end of our service to Him. He
has more in store for us and will provide and protect us during this
part of our journey. How He will use this for good, only time will
tell, but being confident in Him and His promises also gives me
confidence that He will. This confidence, however, only comes
about from being certain of our purpose and God's plan.

Jeremiah 29:11 promises us, "'For I know the plans I have for you,' declares the Lord, 'plans to prosper you and not to harm you, plans to give you hope and a future.'" God's plans for us are for our good and for the good of others. That does not mean though that everything that happens to us will be good; scripture plainly indicates the contrary, as does practical life experience. However, Romans 8:28 reminds us that God will use all things for our good, for our benefit, to help us grow and mature, to be more effective for Him, and to bring Him honor and glory through the whole process. We also need to remember that no matter the bumps in the road, nothing will thwart God's plan and purpose. "For the LORD Almighty has purposed, and who can thwart him? His hand is stretched out, and who can turn it back?" Isaiah 14:27. Our choices can delay His plans, even cause Him to find another person to serve in our place until we get back on track, but He will always find a way for His will to be done.

While we each have a unique calling on our life and a unique role to play, the reason behind it is very much the same: to spread the good news of grace through Jesus Christ. Our calling, our purpose, is our individualized manner through which we fulfill this goal. Our calling can be our vocation: preacher, teacher, soldier, horse trainer, dancer, singer, well driller, welder, mechanic, accountant, doctor, lawyer, the list is infinite. Our calling is the culmination of the God-given talents, gifts, interests, abilities that have been nurtured and honed. We can even have more than one calling, such as a vocation and additional ministries in which we feel led to serve.

Many times the ministries we are most passionate about are not vocations but rather service opportunities done for the sheer joy of serving, like caring for the homeless, volunteering at a women's shelter, fostering children, even serving at church as a volunteer. God will open doors for us to pursue our calling, no matter if it is a vocation or a volunteer role. Even though training and showing are not my vocations, God has given Aria and me many opportunities to point people to Him, both inside and outside of the show ring. During Aria's rehab, through social media, I have been able to share what God has been doing for us, in hopes that it will give hope to others in their journey. Posts about how God has orchestrated events; encouragement He has given me through Scripture, devotions, sermons, friends and family; recurring themes and lessons He has impressed on me; and of course progress reports and occasional videos of Aria at different stages of her rehab, which have allowed Aria to testify on her own of God's goodness and grace. In time, I know God will continue to provide ministry opportunities for us that will allow us to testify to what He has done for us, even though, as of yet, He has not made that our vocation.

No matter what our passion, our calling, and our vocation are, ultimately God gave us all of them so that we could be His hands and feet in this world. Galatians 2:20 says, "I have been crucified with Christ and I no longer life, but Christ lives in me. The life I live in the body, I live by faith in the Son of God, who loved me and gave himself for me." Therefore, no matter our unique calling, the purpose of our calling is to allow Christ to live through us. We are to be His hands, His feet, His voice. We set aside anything in our lives that does not please Him, and we live a life that reflects Him. As we go about our lives, we live out His teachings and His ways. Matthew 5:13-16 tells us to be the salt and light of the world. Salt has no flavor of its own. It only enhances the flavor that is already there. We are to bring out the flavor of God that is already in this world but that people have not been able to taste until our lives and actions draw it out. The same goes with being the light. The light that we have is not our own. 2 Corinthians 4:7 describes us as broken vessels that let God's light and power shine through us. We are to reflect God's light, His love, His grace, His power, through our lives.

We are to reflect God accurately, though. When our lives get dingy with sin, our ability to mirror God gets dingy as well, and we reflect a poor representation of Him. People notice this. While they may not know God well, they have a rough idea of who He is and how those that follow Him are to behave. When we behave contrary to that, we diminish their ability to see the true image of God and may even prevent them from turning to God. Many times we are the only "Jesus" people see, and if they like what they see, then they will want to know more and consider giving their life to Him. However, if they do not like what they see, if we behave in a way that is worse in their eyes than the "good" people they know who are not Christians, in all likelihood they will want absolutely nothing to do with us or the One we claim to represent. And who can blame them? Who would want to be a part of mean spirited, judgmental, condescending people? We have to remember what attracted us to Christ and reflect that accurately in order to attract others to Him. If we have been reflecting a dingy image of God, we, through His grace and forgiveness, have the opportunity to let God clean up our mirror and accurately reflect Him again. Sometimes people have only ever seen dingy reflections of Him, and when they realize this, and they finally get to see who God truly is and what He truly is all about, they may in fact decide they want to be a part of that, the real, true God and His grace after all.

Our lives need to match up with what we say we believe. No one likes to be told "do as I say, not as I do," or to see that concept lived out where people profess to follow Christ but act nothing like Him. Mahatma Gandhi is quoted to have said, "I like your Christ. I do not like your Christians. Your Christians are so unlike your Christ."[7] As heartbreaking as that is, so many times it is true. Our deeds must line up with our faith. James 2:18b-19 says, "Show me your faith without deeds, and I will show you my faith by what I do. You believe that there is but one God. Good! Even the demons believe that—and shudder." It goes back to the fact that God wants a healthy relationship with us. That is the root of our purpose: to have a right relationship with God and encourage others in their own relationship with God. Just believing He exists is not enough. Even Satan believes God exists. He knows God exists. No one would assume that would get Satan into Heaven though. It takes accepting God's grace and giving God control of our life in return in order to pursue His purpose for us and His calling on our lives.

Everything we do, at work, at home, at church, at school, at the barn, in the show ring, anywhere and everywhere, "Whatever you do, work at it with all your heart, as working for the Lord, not for men," Colossians 3:23, for we are in fact working for and with God. "For we are God's fellow workers; you are God's field, God's building." 1 Corinthians 3:9. Note that we are God's FELLOW workers. He does not just give us marching orders and then go sit back in His arm chair and watch us flail about trying to obey them. He works alongside us. Our General, our Boss, is in the trenches with us, guiding us, helping us, giving us clarity and discernment, moment by moment, showing us what we should say or do in any given situation that will best point people to Him.

"But in your hearts set apart Christ as Lord. Always be prepared to give an answer to everyone who asks you to give the reason for the hope that you have. But do this with gentleness and respect, keeping a clear conscience, so that those who speak maliciously against your good behavior in Christ may be ashamed of their slander." 1 Peter 3:15-16. Our lives should be different enough that people notice and want to know why we are different. We should be ready to explain why; that is our purpose. The beautiful thing though is we do not have to have a wrote answer memorized. Matthew 10:19-20 tells us not to worry about what to say or how to say it, that we will be given the words to say when called upon to share Christ to others. A wrote answer will not necessarily fit any given situation, but the Holy Spirit can take our story, our testimony, and help us present it in a way that pricks the heart of the person asking us why we are the way we are. We just need to be ready.

We need to be ready and willing when we hear God say, "Whom shall I send? And who will go for us?" as Isaiah did in chapter 6 verse 8, to answer in like manner: "Here am I. Send me!" Giving God a blank check like that can be incredibly scary, but it is worth it. He knows how best to use every aspect of who we are, where best to place us to make the greatest impact for Him, touching the most hearts and lives, and when best to place us there. We will have the most fulfillment in our life if we surrender our will to His and let Him take the reins. Then, there will come a day when we realize exactly why God put us where He did, when He did, just like Queen Esther did in Esther 4:14 when Mordecai told her, "For if you remain silent at this time, relief and deliverance for the Jews will arise from another place, but you and your father's family will perish. And who knows but that you have come to royal position for such a time as this." For such a time as this. When that moment comes, we have a choice like Esther: be bold and fulfill our purpose, or step back and let someone else do it. Someone else will, but the results will not be as good, as complete, as awe-inspiring as if we, God's first choice, had stepped up to the plate. God will never force us to obey His calling. He has a Plan B if we tell Him no, but Plan B is never as good as Plan A.

"Therefore, since we are surrounded by such a great cloud of witnesses, let us throw off everything that hinders and the sin that so easily entangles, and let us run with perseverance the race marked out for us. Let us fix our eyes on Jesus, the author and perfecter of our faith." Hebrews 12:1-2a. Take special note that not everything that hinders us is sin. Sin is listed entirely separately. Hindrances from running the race God has laid out for us can be incredibly good things, just things that are not for us to do. There is nothing wrong with volunteering at a soup kitchen, but if God's calling for you is to give haircuts to the homeless, hair clippings and pots of soup do not exactly mix. You may be able to do both, but if you find you have to choose, pursue your calling. Those things we have to let go to do what God wants us to do, God has someone already in mind to hand them to. We were His Plan B. We need to step back and let God's Plan A take over. When we stretch ourselves too thin doing too many ministries, jobs, or activities, we cannot adequately do them all. We can actually be doing more harm giving our partial attention to many things instead of devoting our full attention to just a few things. We start dropping the ball in one area or another, and spiritual needs of those we serve are not met as fully as they should. We can also be preventing someone else from having the opportunity to serve as God has called them to. There could be a master chef wanting to make soup for the homeless, but as long as you make soup instead of giving haircuts, the chef sees no need for their skills at the kitchen.

Granted, both of you can make soup, but the homeless would most likely not want the chef giving them haircuts.

If we choose to continue to try to do too much, or serve in a capacity outside of our calling, God will at times take matters into His own hands. In John 15:1-8, Jesus tells us that God removes the branches from the vine that do not bear fruit and prunes those that do. If we are not bearing fruit in a particular role, He may remove us from that role so that it can be filled by someone who is more fruitful. The lack of fruit is evidence that we were serving in a capacity outside of our calling – even though the capacity itself was good. By taking us out of that role, He gives us the opportunity to reflect on Him and the gifts He has given us and discover a way to serve that we had not considered before and is a much better fit for us. Once we step into that new role, we begin producing abundantly for God. If we were fruitful in a role we have lost, the God is pruning us and positioning us for a new opportunity we would have otherwise been unable to fill. In this new role, we can take the experience gained from our previous position and become even more fruitful.

God used the spiritual warfare around 2017 World as a means to prune in my life. It forced me to reassess the many roles of service I had on my plate at the time. He allowed me to see which ones I had been doing because I was called to them and which ones I was doing simply to fill the need. He also helped me see where I was called to certain aspects of certain roles but not called to other aspects. Ultimately, He pruned me from one body of believers and grafted me into another, one that allows me to serve as I am truly called and encourages me in those areas of service. The difference is astounding. The process was painful and difficult, but absolutely necessary. God knew I needed to be moved to a different part of His vine in order to freely grow and bear fruit. He knew that unless the section of vine I had been apart of kept cutting away at my calling until there was nothing left for me there, I would not have been able to be grafted to where I was truly needed and wanted. It took time, but that time was needed to heal from the wounds of the spiritual warfare I had been through.

Sometimes your new opportunity does not follow closely on the heels of the old one, just like mine did not, and you find yourself in the wilderness of waiting, just like I did. Use this time to grow deeper roots in Christ. This too will make you more fruitful in the coming days. Deeper roots encourage outward growth, making you more capable spiritually, mentally, and emotionally for whatever capacity God will lead you to serve in the future. Get to know the heart of God even more intimately during this time. God has removed the distractions of being busy for Him so that you can sit at His feet and focus on Him. When Martha was upset that Mary was sitting at Jesus's feet, listening to Him teach, rather than helping her, Jesus told her, "you are worried and upset about many things, but only one thing is needed. Mary has chosen what is better, and it will not be taken away from her." Luke 10:41-42. Learn from Martha and be like Mary. Focus on Him first. Listen to

Him first. Then do for Him. Not the other way around. When we cannot learn to do that on our own, He will eliminate our busyness for us. Many times that is the reason behind a time of waiting: to reset our focus and our priorities.

Encourage others as they serve God in their unique calling. This can be just as important as living out your purpose. In fact, encouraging others to pursue their callings can actually be your calling. Everyone one of us knows what a difference a well-timed, heartfelt, kind, uplifting word can make. We need encouragers in our lives, in our families, in our churches, in our communities. It is a vital, often overlooked role, but one that is crucial in the big picture of God's plan. Encouragers are the ones that God uses to keep us going, to refill the empty cup of our spirit, to help renew us so that we can be at our best and serve God as He wants us to. The encouragement God has provided me has been invaluable in this journey with Aria. Whether it came directly through His Word and His Spirit or through the encouragement of other believers, it has bolstered my faith, provided much needed clarity, guidance, and hope. Without it, this road would have been so much more difficult. It has renewed my desire to be encouraging to others, for I see both how much it is needed and how in short supply it can be.

Encouragers are incredibly important and can make a greater impact that they realize at first. A perfect example is "Joseph, a Levite from Cyprus, whom the apostles called Barnabas (which means 'son of encouragement')." Acts 4:36. According to Acts 9:27, if it were not for Barnabas's testimony about Saul, later known as Paul, the apostles would not have accepted him. He served along side Paul, offering encouragement and support to Paul, until Paul refused to show grace to John (also known as Mark, who, we learn in Colossians 4:10, was Barnabas's cousin) when Barnabas wanted to give Mark a second chance to minister with them after Mark had chosen to leave them for a time. They disagreed so divisively that they parted ways, Barnabas leaving with Mark to serve together and Paul leaving with Silas. This is recorded in Acts 15:36-41. I have always wondered how the perception of Christianity would have been shaped differently had the Son of Encouragement had a longer influence on Paul. Would it still be seen as judgmental and condescending or would it be seen as gracious and encouraging as Christ intended? We will never know. What we do know is Barnabas's influence on Mark inspired the young man to sell out to Christ completely and make just as lasting of an impact for Him as Paul, as evidenced by the fact we have a Gospel attributed to Mark. Even though we do not have all the details of Mark's growth or of his and Barnabas's ministry together, Barnabas obviously saw potential in Mark that Paul missed, and through Barnabas's encouragement, that potential became reality. In all likelihood, that growth would not have ever happened had Barnabas not taken a stand and stood up for Mark against Paul, at the cost of his friendship with Paul and of being a part of a well-known ministry. Being an encourager often times means stepping out of the limelight so that others can shine, like Barnabas did for Mark. Sometimes

God asks you to take a stand in someone's defense when no one else seems to have their back, even at great cost to you. But the eternal benefits of being an encourager outweigh all of that.

From our vantage point, we cannot see how everyone's purposes fit together, but we know that God designed each of us with a unique purpose that fits perfectly with the unique purposes of everyone else in His family. Each and every person's purpose is crucial to God's overall plan. Our individual purpose works in harmony with those of others to accomplish our collective purpose: to share the Gospel and God's grace to a lost and dying world. Like in a musical composition, different melodies take the forefront at different times, harmonizing together, the one in the background encouraging the one in the foreground, and vice versa as the melodies' roles change. In order to see how our unique melody harmonizes with the melody of others, we need to delve into God's Word and stay in His presence so that we can accurately hear the pitches that are ours and ours alone. We need to consult the Composer to make sure we have our part of the harmony correct. Doing so encourages consonance rather than dissonance within the body of Christ. We need to be sure of our purpose so that we can be of the greatest benefit to the family of God and so that we can be in alignment with God's will for our lives.

Points to Ponder...

- What is your vocation? How can God use you within that role to spread the Gospel and point people to Him? If you cannot openly witness at your job, how else can you serve Him there?

- What are you passionate about? How might that passion be the budding of your calling? How might your character traits and talents be used by God to bring Him glory?

- Is there anything you need to set aside to more effectively serve God? What steps can you take to keep yourself from getting stretched too thin?

Chapter 9

God's Perspective of Our Circumstances

"And we know that in all things God works for the good of those who love him, who have been called according to his purpose."
Romans 8:28

As Hebrews 12:1-2 point out, God has a path, a race, laid out for each of us to run. There will be hindrances, entanglements, times we stumble and fall or get distracted and sidetracked, but if we stay focused on Jesus, He will get us back on track, and we will persevere. This path He has us on will be more incredible than we could ever hope or imagine. "However, as it is written: 'No eye has seen, no ear has heard, no mind has conceived what God has prepared for those who love him.' — but God has revealed it to us by his Spirit. The Spirit searches all things, even the deep things of God." 1 Corinthians 2:9-10. God will not lay out for us the whole path, His entire plan for our lives, because we would be completely overwhelmed if He did. He will, however, reveal what we need to know when we need to know it. In those times of waiting for clarity, for His perspective of our circumstances, we can take great comfort in Ephesians 3:20-21. "Now to him who is able to do immeasurably more than all we ask or imagine, according to his power that is at work within us, to Him be the glory in the church and in Christ Jesus throughout all generations, for ever and ever! Amen." Right now, at this very moment, God can handle the circumstances around us in a way that is absolutely beyond our wildest dreams. Yes, just because He can [insert your desired solution to your present circumstance], does not mean that He will; HOWEVER, just because He hasn't, doesn't mean that He won't. What is certain is He WILL work in your circumstance in a way that will bring Him honor and glory for generations and in a way that is best for you and those involved. It will be one of those stories of His power that gets handed down from one generation to the next. Those Red Sea moments only He can handle…and does. Yes, God could immediately, instantly, and completely heal Aria, but as of yet, He has not. That does not mean that He will not heal her. It means that the way He is going about it will bring Him more honor and glory than if He had instantly healed her. For one thing, because it is taking time for her to heal, I will appreciate her being whole all the more than if we had just been sidelined for a few days. I see that it is not by my power or the vet's alone that she will get well. It will be by the hand of God. He is using the vet and me to help her heal, but ultimately, the actual act of healing is on Him. His power is at work at this very moment in our respective circumstances, behind the scenes, and within us. When we cannot see it or feel it, like when I cannot see improvement in Aria's leg from one day to the next, these verses give us something to lean on. He IS able, and He IS working, and He IS willing to do what is best for us and what will bring Him the most glory. It just takes time to see all of this plays out.

Part of my underlying fear around Aria's injury and my desire for God to heal her lay in the knowledge that I had repeatedly, incessantly, prayed for God to heal both Momma and Blue. For both, He said no, not in this life. Both Momma and Blue are fully healthy, fully whole again in Heaven, but that was not the answer I had wanted. I wanted them restored in THIS life, so that they would still be with me, for years to come. But God said no. I knew full well that just because God can, does not mean that He will. He could have easily healed both Momma and Blue, but He chose not to, for reasons I may never fully comprehend until I too am in Heaven. My fear was that since He had said no to healing Momma and Blue, that He would continue the pattern and say no to healing Aria. I could not bear that thought. I felt like the father in Mark 9 who came to Jesus to have the evil spirit cast out of his son. When Jesus said, "'Everything is possible for one who believes.' Immediately the boy's father exclaimed, 'I do believe; help me overcome my unbelief!'" Mark 9:23b-24. The father knew Jesus was fully capable of healing his son. He believed in Jesus's power. His unbelief was that he just was not sure Jesus would actually heal his son. No one else could help him, so he had his doubts that maybe Jesus would not be willing to help either. Just because Jesus had healed loved ones for others, did not mean He would heal his son for him. I knew Jesus could heal Aria. Like the boy's father, I believe in His power, and, like the father, I needed help overcoming my unbelief that Jesus might be unwilling to heal her, that He might not heal her for me, simply because it was me asking. Slowly through my fear, a Still, Small Voice reminded me, "just because I haven't, doesn't mean that I won't." Just because God has not answered my prayers of healing as I have wanted before does not mean that He will not this time. Just because God did not heal Momma and Blue does not mean He will not heal Aria. As my fear was replaced with hope, He led me to Psalm 27:13-14. "I am still confident of this: I will see the goodness of the LORD in the land of the living. Wait for the LORD; be strong and take heart and wait for the LORD." I will see God's grace and healing of Aria in THIS life. I just have to wait for Him to move and heal her when He deems best. While I wait, I lean on Him for strength and find comfort in His promises and in His presence.

Remember, Romans 8:28 promises that God will make good come from all things for those that love Him and are called according to His purpose. When we are doing all we can to follow His leading, pursuing His calling and purpose for our life, we can trust that the rough patches we hit will be used for good. The verse does not say "all things are good," but that God can and will bring good from the bad. Like that old saying, "every cloud has a silver lining." When in uncertain circumstances, start looking for the good. No situation is all bad, and if we pray through it, God will give us glimpses of how He is going to use the situation and of what we are to learn from it. Doing this will help shift our whole mindset and give us a new perspective. His perspective.

While the spiritual warfare around World was intense and heartbreaking, ultimately God used it to get me out of a bad situation and lead me to a loving, Christ-centered, encouraging church family that has been instrumental in my healing and growth in this wilderness. They have celebrated alongside me as Aria's healing progressed and offered encouragement and sympathy when she had backsets. The spiritual warfare was not good, but God worked good from it. I would have never found my way to that church had it not been for that time of darkness.

One way God has already used Aria's injury for good is by bringing a new pup into my life. Because of our weekly trips to the vet for laser therapy, I have gotten to know the vet and his staff well, counting them now as friends. The vet tech, Teri, was fostering a young mini Australian Shepherd named Shorty. She had taken him in from a client who had surrendered him due to no longer being able to care for him. Teri had asked me if I knew of anyone who might be interested in adopting him, but offhand I could not think of anyone and I was not ready for another dog. Blue left a big hole in my heart that I was not sure I wanted to fill. A few weeks passed, and she still had not found him a forever home. She had him at the clinic, so I decided to meet him. She warned me that Shorty tended to bark at folks when he first met them, but when she let him out of the kennel, Shorty ran right up to me, excited and wanting love, but not one bark. We took him outside, and he ran around the trailer and sniffed at Aria inside, but no barking at her either. Shorty was a sweetheart, but I just was not ready for another dog.

After we left, I could not get Shorty out of my mind. Finally I decided if he gets along with Aria and with Daddy, we would take him home. First, though, we had to fix the backyard fence. We had moved part of the fence for Blue to make her a small yard, so she could enjoy freedom and the outdoors her final few months without being able to wander too far from the house. I wanted to keep Blue's small yard intact, for it would be handy if we needed to leave Shorty outside while we were not home. So, we measured how much material we needed to repair the fence to the rest of the backyard so that Shorty would have more room to run and play outside of Blue's small yard. We went over to my grandparents' place where we had some wire panels that would easily fix the fence. We measured the panels, and we were a foot short. We went ahead and brought the panels to the house, figuring we could makeshift the balance. We set up the panels, and lo and behold, a perfect fit! Sure, you could say we mismeasured one or the other, but I say God provided, and I took it as Him saying He wanted me to adopt Shorty.

Our next appointment was the true test. I let Aria hand-graze behind the clinic, and Teri let Shorty out. He ran by Aria, and neither batted an eye. Aria kept grazing without a care in the world as Shorty checked her out cautiously. When he saw she accepted him, they were instant siblings, good friends, but they have been known to pick on each other. The final test was how he reacted to Daddy, for Shorty was not very trusting of men. Shorty ran up to Daddy without a single bark, greeted him, and then took off playing again. The clencher for Daddy was when Shorty was on the far side of the lot behind the clinic, and when Daddy called him, Shorty came running back without hesitation. Shorty went home with us that day, and he rode in my lap the whole way home. He still loves to ride in my lap, and he and Aria still get along incredibly well, though both of their herding instincts do kick in from time to time, and they end up chasing each other's tail.

Shorty has been such a blessing to both Daddy and me, bringing much needed joy and laughter into our home. He has been great at the barn, learning the ropes quickly and accompanying Aria and I on our rides. When Aria is stopped, she lets Shorty run underneath her. He will pop up on his hindlegs for a pet, sometimes balancing against my foot, sometimes against Aria's shoulder. The only time she fusses at him is when he cuts too close when we are moving, which makes sense. She does not want to accidently hurt him. Shorty has also learned how to help herd Aria to where I need her. If she is reluctant to move when I ask her to on the ground, Shorty will run up to her. He will pause to see if that is enough to get her to move. If not, he will bark and tap her hindlegs with his nose. She never tries to kick him, but she will occasionally swat him with her tail in protest as she moves like he tells her to. God knew that all of us, Aria, Daddy, me, and Shorty, needed each other and orchestrated events, including Aria's injury, to bring us all together.

I did not realize how much orchestration was involved until I started looking through the papers Teri had given me on Shorty. His breeder was in the Houston area, as were the family who purchased him. They could not keep him, so they passed him along to another woman in the area. She too surrendered him at some point, and somehow he ended up in Denton County, where he was adopted, sent to a rescue, rescued from the rescue, and then surrendered to the vet, before he found his forever home with us. I realized then that if God could orchestrate Shorty's path so that he ended up in my life at the perfect time, even when I did not know I needed him, then God could most definitely handle perfectly orchestrating all the other areas of my life, if I just stay out of His way and let Him.

It is incredibly easy to get overwhelmed, fearful, even doubt God's goodness and presence in difficult times when you are waiting for His orchestration to pan out. I know this because I have been there. 2 Timothy 1:7 (NKJV) reminds us, though, "For God has not given us a spirit of fear, but of power and of love and of a sound mind." The NIV translates "sound mind" as "self-discipline." It takes quite a bit of self-discipline to shift our mindset from one of fear and apprehension to one of power and love, one of God's peace. Fortunately, Paul gave us a road map to shifting our perspective and accessing God's peace in Philippians 4:8-9. He said, "Finally, brothers, whatever is true, whatever is noble, whatever is right, whatever is pure, whatever is lovely, whatever is admirable — if anything is excellent or praiseworthy — think about such things.

Whatever you have learned or received or heard from me, or seen in me—put into practice. And the peace of God will be with you." In other words, quit the stinkin' thinkin'. Spend time in His presence. When our thoughts turn dark, turn to Him to shed light on them so that we can see our circumstances from His view point. Dive into God's Word. Turn to trusted Godly friends for counsel. Both help shift our thoughts from fear to what is right, true, noble, pure, lovely, admirable, excellent, and praiseworthy. Peace naturally follows when our focus is on the good and on the Light.

This may not change our circumstance any, but changing the way we look at it will make it more bearable, and we can start to see God's hand at work in it. We have to remember, as Isaiah 55:8-9 points out, that God's ways are not our ways. His timing is not our timing. His ways, His timing, are so much better, so much greater than ours that the only comparison is how much higher the heavens are than the earth. God sees us as He saw Hagar in her dire straits in Genesis 16, as He saw Joseph in Genesis 37-50. He does not just see us now, but He also sees where He needs us in the future. He allows events to unfold in ways that may not make sense at the time, in ways that may even be painful, so that we end up right where He needs us in the future, each circumstance molding our character to be like His so that in His perfect timing, we are in the right place at the right time to accomplish the right things. As Joseph said in Genesis 50:20, "You intended to harm me, but God intended it for good to accomplish what is now being done, the saving of many lives." Hopefully, none of us are thrown into a pit, sold as a slave, falsely accused and imprisoned as Joseph was, but there will be times we feel like we are in a pit or have been sold out or lied about. Those times will hurt, but they will also be times of growth, growth required to accomplish God's purpose for us. God will use the bad to accomplish good.

Like with Joseph's life, sometimes it takes a long time to see how all the pieces fit together, but at some point we will see how God uses our present circumstances. When things start falling together, hang on tight because God will start moving quickly. Isaiah 60:22b says, "I am the Lord; in its time I will do this swiftly." It may seem like God is moving slowly, or not even working at all, much like those days when it seems like Aria is not improving. These are the times God is working behind the scenes, moving all the pieces into place before He can visibly move in our lives, just like Aria's deep tissues must heal behind the scenes where I cannot see before there is change and healing to her leg that I can see. This is when faith is absolutely crucial. "Now faith is being sure of what we hope for and certain of what we do not see." Hebrews 11:1. All the time we spend in God's presence, all the time we spend transforming and renewing our mind (Romans 12:2), it deposits into our faith, our ability to trust that God's promises apply to us. We adopt His mindset and His perspective on our lives and trust that God is working on our behalf, even when at the moment we see no evidence of it. It gives us confidence that even though God is quiet, He is still there. He is still healing Aria even when I cannot see it. When our situation looks bleak, He will still work good from it.

These are the times of trials and testing. These are the times we are tempted to fall back into the thought patterns of the world. However, "Do not conform any longer to the pattern of this world, but be transformed by the renewing of your mind. Then you will be able to test and approve what God's will is—his good, pleasing, and perfect will." Romans 12:2. We renew our mind by entering God's presence, spending time in His Word and in prayer. That is the only way to learn and know the mind of God, His character, and His ways. Only by knowing Him can we truly know His will. Then we can start to see His hand in our circumstances. We see His provision, His protection, and how He helps us persevere. So, hang in there. As my grandfather always said, "the darkest hour is just before dawn."

Points to Ponder...

- Think about some dark times in your life. At the time, could you see God's hand working things for good? If not, can you now see it, looking back on the situation? How so?

- How have you seen God's orchestration in your life, both in large ways and in small ones?

- What is a current situation in your life that you know God can handle, but you are not sure He will? What are some active steps you can take to allow God to change your perspective and give you hope?

Chapter 10

Provision

"Ask and it will be given to you; seek and you will find;
knock and the door will be opened to you."
Matthew 7:7

Billy Graham once said, "The will of God will not take us where the grace of God cannot sustain us."[8] As we pursue God's will for our lives, the circumstances and trials we face not only shape us into the individuals God wants us to be and position us where He needs us, but they also provide God the opportunity to show us and those around us His divine provision. We have needs only He can meet, and He will provide. In the Sermon on the Mount, Jesus addresses our concerns for our physical needs in Matthew 6:25-34. He reminds us that God makes sure all the animals and plants are fed, watered, and protected from the elements. If He does this for them, He will do the same for us. However, there is a stipulation. Matthew 6:33 says, "But seek first his kingdom and his righteousness, and all these things will be given to you as well." We have to be pursuing God, following His leading, striving to be men and women of Godly character before He will grant us His provision. He is not going to bless our efforts if our efforts are not bless-able. He is not going to provide if we just sit back and expect Him to just drop food, clothing, and shelter in our laps either. We have to do our part. Granted, we can do all we can, doing our best to follow God and live as He wants us to, and things can still go sideways, and circumstances out of our control put us in a position that we have no idea where our next meal will come from or how we will keep a roof over our heads. God sees this and is aware of our needs in these situations. He will still provide, sometimes miraculously by groceries appearing on the doorstep or an unexpected check in the mail, and sometimes He provides by showing us where to turn for help. That is also one of the functions of the body of believers. We should be willing to step up and be instruments of God's provision when we are able to help meet the needs of others.

The Bible gives us examples of God providing in all these manners. In Exodus 16 and 17, God provided manna and quail for the Israelites. It literally fell out of the sky and landed in their camp. He provided water from a rock. The Creator has no problem creating, literally, a solution to our physical need, but only if that is the best route to provide for us that also allows us to glean the most spiritual benefits and gives Him the most glory. In John 6:1-15, Jesus chose to use a young boy to meet a great physical need. The boy did not have much to offer Jesus, just a small lunch, but he gave it willingly. Jesus blessed the boy's gift and multiplied it to feed five thousand men and an unknown number of women and children. We may not feel like we have much to offer God, but when we willingly give God what we have, in His hands, He can take it and work miracles. The results of any gift, of anything we do in His name, are always up to God. Our responsibility is to simply do, give, obey, and leave the rest in His more than capable hands. We have no idea the long term, even eternal, results God works from our one act of obedience. One bag of groceries given to a family in need could be the encouragement the parents need to keep trying. One phone call could interrupt a person's dark thoughts, reminding them they are not alone and giving them courage to go on living. One smile at a stranger may brighten their entire day. Our actions are like tossing a stone into a pond. We may not see the ripples triggered by our one act and how far reaching the effect actually is. That family we give the groceries to may be inspired to open a community pantry to help other families in need. That person whose life we unknowingly saved may decide to be strong and seek counseling and encourage others to see the strength in reaching out for help, saving countless other lives. The stranger we smiled at may go into a meeting with a much more positive outlook and agree to helping fund youth centers and parks in low income areas, giving numerous kids a safe place to play and hang out. Each act of obedience inspiring another and another. Ripples touching more and more lives as they radiate out. All because we are willing to give God the little we have to offer.

I may never know the effect of the ripples created by Aria and me obediently following God's leading to APHA World, by Him moving in a mighty way so that we won, by the glory He has received from it. Right after our World Championship, I was interviewed by Kristen Weaver for KXII News[9], one of our local television stations, and by Alana Harrison for the Paint Horse Journal[10], APHA's monthly publication that goes world-wide. In both interviews, I was able to give God credit and share how He worked in this experience and showed up in a mighty way. Then, in the spring, my hometown honored me by giving me the key to the city. This prompted Bill Douglass of Douglass Distributing to ask for a picture of Aria and me from World to have professionally mounted and hung where the public could see our accomplishment. This too allowed me to share with him about how God's hand has been in this. This picture was hung in our local Subway restaurant on Momma's birthday. The timing was further proof of God's guidance in this journey. It was a beautiful tribute to her as well, the perfect birthday present. I have no doubt she was beaming from ear to ear in Heaven as she watched them hang our picture. This again gave me the chance to remind people just Who is truly responsible for our success and once again give Him the glory. The picture was later moved from Subway to the entrance of the adjoining gas station to provide increased visibility. I am incredibly grateful for each of these opportunities that God has granted me to use our World Championship to point people to Him. I want people to know that this journey always has and always will be about Him and what He can do, not me and what I can do. If our story can inspire just one young girl or young boy to chase the dreams God has given them, if we can encourage just one person to turn to God from seeing how awesome and powerful and gracious

He is, for the first time or to renew their relationship with Him, then that is a mighty miracle orchestrated from our act of obedience.

The same goes for Aria's injury. If we can inspire just one person to realize that just because they have been hurt, emotionally or physically, even severely, that does not mean they are down for the count, and life is over, and if we can help them see that God can still use them if they let Him show them how to improvise, adapt, and overcome, then this wilderness experience will be worth all the heartache and tears it has caused. Maybe as you read this, you will be motivated by our journey and step out on faith and chase your God-sized dream. If so, consider me your biggest cheerleader, and know that I am humbled to be a part of your journey to the Promised Land God has in store for you, to be a part of the miracles He works in your life. Maybe as you face your wilderness, you will be encouraged to keep forging ahead as you see how God is working in Aria's and my wilderness. If so, know that I am praying for you and that you see God's hand of provision and guidance in your own situation.

Sometimes God allows us to be in physical need to steer us in a different direction of service that will not only provide for our needs, but also better suits our calling and purpose. As long as we are comfortable, we do not see any need in changing jobs or career paths, even if we feel like eventually God wants us to do something different. We tell ourselves we will do that later when we have the time, or when the kids are older, or after we are promoted, or some other point in time. While these can be very valid reasons to hold off on a dream God has given us, for instance if you are helping pay for two kids to go through college, going back to college yourself may not be financially feasible at the moment, but sometimes God has something else in mind for us. Sometimes "eventually" needs to be "right now" because of how our piece of the puzzle fits in with the pieces of others, and ours needs to be in the proper place before theirs can be put into place. So, God shakes things up. That job we were comfortable in suddenly gets downsized. That one-bedroom apartment we have will not be big enough when the baby arrives. Suddenly, we are having to consider options we would have never considered before. New jobs. New opportunities. New careers. New homes. New neighborhoods. All moving us in a direction we had not planned, but putting us in the perfect place to pursue that "eventual" dream God planted in our hearts that will blossom and flourish, blessing more than just us but also all those around where God places us. Nudging us to push past comfortable into the realm of complete and utter trust in God and His provision and into whatever lies beyond the unexpected change is a unique opportunity to bring God glory and to serve Him in a way we could not have if He had left us in our comfort zone.

Knowing what to do, where to turn, and how to proceed can be difficult, but "If any of you lacks wisdom, he should ask God, who gives generously to all without finding fault, and it will be given to him." James 1:5. When we have no clue what to do, or need discernment as to which path to take, or need wisdom in how to handle a situation, we need to ask God for wisdom. God is more than willing to answer that prayer with a resounding affirmative. Wisdom and discernment are crucial to knowing what God wants and expects, so God will provide them without hesitation when we need them. How else will we know God's will? He will never fault us or shame us for needing more wisdom. First, asking Him for wisdom acknowledges our limitations and His abundance. It shows humility and a contrite heart, characteristics God readily approves. Secondly, Godly wisdom better equips us to face anything life throws at us. The better equipped we are, the better the likelihood we will respond to circumstances in a way that honors and pleases God. Therefore, of course He will grant us wisdom. He provides that wisdom through His Word and through THE Word, Jesus. The Holy Spirit will guide us to passages that speak to our needs and will emphasize aspects of the Christ and His teachings that help us know what to do. Any path He wants us to take and any decision He wants us to make will line up perfectly with the guidelines in His Word. Anything that falls outside of His Word and His ways falls outside of His will as well. It circles back to spending time with Him and in His Word to learn His character and discern the wisest plan of action in His eyes.

When needing guidance, it is important to completely trust God and His wisdom rather than our own. Proverbs 3:5-6 says, "Trust in the LORD with all your heart and lean not on your own understanding; in all your ways acknowledge him and he will make your paths straight." In other words, trust God with all areas of our lives, put Him first, and give Him all the credit. Then He will make it clear what He wants for us and from us. He will make the path clear, not easy, but straightforward. "See, I am doing a new thing! Now it springs up; do you not perceive it? I am making a way in the desert and streams in the wasteland." Isaiah 43:19. Our journey through life many times feels like a wilderness experience, wandering around, looking for direction, like the Israelites did. Remember, even when we do not see God work, even when we feel like we are wandering in circles, He IS working, He IS blazing a trail for us, and He WILL provide direction once He has all the work behind the scenes completed. No one wants to cross the desert until the streams are in place and the trail secure. Getting ahead of God like that is a recipe for disaster. He will give us glimpses of His handiwork to give us hope and fuel our faith, and when the time is right, He will take us by the hand and lead us to our earthly Promised Land.

A crucial provision God grants us as we journey through life with Him is His perfect peace. Isaiah 26:3 tells us, "You will keep in perfect peace him whose mind is steadfast, because He trusts in you." Paul goes on to say in Philippians 4:4-7, "Rejoice in the Lord always. I will say it again: Rejoice! Let your gentleness be evident to all. The Lord is near. Do not be anxious about anything, but in everything by prayer and petition, with thanksgiving, present your requests to God. And the peace of God, which transcends all understanding, will guard your hearts and minds in Christ Jesus." Our hearts and minds are easy targets in uncertain times. That is why it is imperative to allow God's peace to guard both. God provides His peace when we fully trust Him, fully believing that He has our best interest at heart, and will truly provide what is best for us. This gives us assurance that no matter what life looks like now, God hears our requests and will answer them when the time is right. Knowing God is steadfast and trustworthy comes about from time in His presence and Word. Peace comes from knowing we and our lives are in the best possible hands. This peace keeps dark thoughts of doubt and despair at bay, even in the roughest of times. They may creep in, attempting to get a toe hold, but God's truth will drive them out if we listen to His voice over theirs.

In our times of hardship, when we feel weak and helpless, that is when Christ's strength and power become all the more evident to us and to those around us. "But he said to me, 'My grace is sufficient for you, for my power is made perfect in weakness.' Therefore, I will boast all the more gladly about my weaknesses, so that Christ's power may rest on me." 2 Corinthians 12:9. God's grace and power will sustain us, even in our weakest moments. Our weakness gives us the ability to point others to the One who sustains us. It gives us a platform upon which we can testify to His grace and provision. When given the opportunity to share our testimony of God's hand in our lives, God will grant us the words to say. "The LORD said to him, 'Who gave man his mouth? Who makes him deaf or mute? Who gives him sight or makes him blind? Is it not I, the LORD? Now go, I will help you speak and will teach you what to say.'" Exodus 4:11-12. Jesus reiterated this when He said, "When you are brought before synagogues, rulers and authorities, do not worry about how you will defend yourselves or what you will say, for the Holy Spirit will teach you at that time what you should say." Luke 12:11-12. No matter if the person asking questions of us is genuinely seeking God or seeking to persecute us, God, through the Holy Spirit, will give us the ability to address their concerns and answer their questions.

Remember, the Holy Spirit will also give us guidance when the issue at hand has no clear precedent in the Bible. In John 16:12-16, Jesus tells us there is more that we need to know than what He taught while on earth, simply because the sheer volume of what all He knows we need to learn would have caused information overload. Therefore, the Holy Spirit's job is to guide us to all truth. He will share with us what He has heard from God and will reveal what is to come in our lives, meaning He will make it clear what we need to know, when we need to know it. Anything He says will be corroborated by Scriptures and will be relevant to us and our present circumstances. Again, the only way to clearly distinguish His voice is to spend time with God and learn His character.

As we do, like we discussed earlier, our heart will align with His. We will want what He wants. We will delight in Him and His ways. Psalm 37:4 says, "Delight yourself in the LORD and He will give you the desires of your heart." This is because the more time we spend with Him, the more we become like Him, and the more our desires will line up with His desires. We will see that He wants only what is best for us, and as we see we can trust His judgement in what is best and what is not, we learn to want His will, His desires, for our life. When the desires of our heart are for the desires of His heart to be done, then naturally He will provide them. He wants His will to be done in our lives, and He is delighted when we allow Him free rein to orchestrate what is best for us. The same goes for Matthew 7:7, "Ask it will be given you; seek and you will find; knock and the door will be opened to you." Jesus goes on to say in verse 11, "If you, then, though you are evil, know how to give good gifts to your children, how much more will your Father in heaven give good gifts to those who ask him!" When our mind is steadfast on God, and our heart is aligned with His, what we ask and seek will also be in accordance with God's will. The opportunities we pursue, the doors we knock on, will be doors God wishes to open. God only wants the best for us, so when what we ask, seek, and pursue are for our good, He will grant our requests. This is because "…my God will meet all your needs according to His glorious riches in Christ Jesus." Philippians 4:19. God will provide our needs, not necessarily our wants, but our needs.

Knowing this fills us with peace and also grants us a measure of freedom. "Now the Lord is the Spirit, and where the Spirit of the Lord is, there is freedom." 2 Corinthians 3:17. This freedom comes from knowing our life is in His hands. It is not on us to make the opportunities appear or to force God's will to happen. We let God be God, working at His pace, orchestrating everything perfectly in

His time, molding us as He sees fit. Trying to do it all ourselves is a burden we were never meant to bear. Letting God be God frees us, frees us to praise Him and worship Him for all He has done and is doing on our behalf, frees us to follow Him, to trust Him, frees us to be who He created us to be, His child and His friend.

Points to Ponder...

- How have you seen God provide for your needs in the past? How does this give you hope in your present situation?

- How has God used changes and challenges in your life to position you to serve Him better or differently?

- What are some ways you feel God nudging you to help provide for the needs of others?

Chapter 11

Protection

"I will say of the LORD, 'He is my refuge and my fortress,
my God, in whom I trust."
Psalm 91:2

As our Father and Friend, God naturally is very protective of us and will do all He can, all that we will allow Him to do, to keep us safe. Psalm 91 is filled with promises of God's protection. We are covered by His wings. His faithfulness is our shield. There is no need to fear threats by night or day. "A thousand may fall at your side, ten thousand at your right hand, but it will not come near you." (v. 7). "If you make the Most High your dwelling – even the LORD, who is my refuge – then no harm will befall you, no disaster will come near your tent. For he will command his angels concerning you to guard you in all your ways; they will lift you up in their hands, so that you will not strike your foot against a stone." (vv. 9-12). While God promises to protect us, that does not mean we are given free license to take unnecessary risks with life and limb. This passage is the very one Satan quoted in Matthew 4:5-6 when he tried to get Jesus to jump off of the highest point of the temple. In verse 7, Jesus gave the perfect rebuttal: "It was also written: 'Do not put the LORD your God to the test.'" In other words, do not do something in an attempt to intentionally make God keep His promises, particularly that of protection.

God's promises to keep us safe apply to when we are acting in accordance with His will and when those whose actions would directly affect our safety are in step with Him as well. His ability to protect extends only as far as free will -- our ability to freely choose our actions, behaviors, attitudes, and so forth -- allows. For instance, if we see a child wander into a busy street, God will protect both us and the child as we run to the rescue, as long as both of us and the drivers make wise decisions in the process. If we time our dash to the child amidst the traffic, and the drivers are alert and can brake and swerve as needed, all will be well. But if we choose to not pay attention to the traffic or drivers choose to not pay attention to the road, there is only so much God can do. Vehicles can only stop so fast. People can only react so fast. Yes, God is sovereign and can do anything; however, He chooses to respect our free will and our decisions, as well as those of others. That is what a loving God does. A controlling god would force people to behave a certain way and make decisions as he saw fit, guaranteeing a perfect outcome, but there is no love in that. Love means showing someone the best option before them and then letting them decide for themselves what to do. Even if that means they choose incorrectly. Yes, God could in His omnipotence and omniscience prevent senseless violence and loss of innocent lives, but to do so would prevent someone from using their free will. Free will is a gift from God, and God does not take His gifts back. Love does not do that. To do so would go against His character and His design of allowing each person to choose for themselves whether or not to follow Him. Where there is no choice, there is no love…not on the part of the one who forces the behavior nor on the part of the one from whom the behavior was forced. This is one of the reasons why bad things happen to good people – because good people are affected by the bad choices of others.

Also, because this world is fallen, disease, injury and disaster happen. God did not give Momma pulmonary hypertension as punishment, just like He did not injure Aria as punishment to me or Aria. Yes, God is sovereign and could have prevented Aria's injury (though she too has free will and chose to do whatever she did that led to her getting hurt), and He could have made sure Momma's DNA was disease free. He could stop hurricanes, tornadoes, earthquakes, tsunamis, or any other natural disaster. He could prevent or cure childhood diseases, birth defects, cancer, Alzheimer's, Parkinson's, and every other disorder or condition of every kind known to man. Sometimes God does intervene in a miraculous way…turning storms or bringing complete and instant healing, but not always. Why He does sometimes and sometimes He does not, I do not know. Maybe nature itself has some degree of free will that while He is sovereign, He cannot interfere. Maybe sometimes He gets more glory through the miracle, and sometimes He gets more glory in how we handle Him not granting us the miracle. Only in His sovereignty would He know that. What I do know is that, whatever happens to us and those we love, He can and will work good from it. While He can only protect us physically as far as we allow and as far as the actions of others allow, He will ALWAYS offer to protect us spiritually. We just have to take Him up on it.

He knows that we will not only face trials and uncertain circumstances, but that we will also face full on battles. When we strive to put Him first ahead of all else and diligently follow His leading, giving Him glory for all our accomplishments, spiritual resistance and attacks will flare up around us, even from the seemingly most unlikely of sources. When Aria and I set our sights on giving God glory at World, I knew Satan would fight back trying to thwart us, but the tactics and the people he used to try to distract us were surprising. However, my prayer became based on Exodus 14:14, asking the Lord to fight for us, to handle the diversionary fire fights, and to give us the strength and focus we needed to perform to the best of our ability, a performance that would honor Him, asking Him to show up and bless our efforts. Our World Championship in Amateur SPB Hunt Seat Equitation and our 3rd in Open SPB Ranch Riding the following week, which was after a particularly difficult onslaught the night before, these honors are proof that God did fight for us and kept the enemy at bay. If God will fight for me, then He will fight for you in your situation as well.

There is no better depiction of the warfare we face and how God equips us than in Ephesians 6:10-18. Priscilla Shirer's study[2] of this passage about the Armor of God contains a treasure trove of insight that I drew upon during World. It heightened my awareness of spiritual warfare, allowing me to recognize it for what it is, and deepened my understanding of all God has granted me to oppose it. I am grateful God guided me to her study because things might have gone much differently during that time had I not listened to Him speak through her.

God calls us to be strong in His might, not our own, and put on His armor in order to be able to stand firm against Satan's attacks. "For our struggle is not against flesh and blood, but against the rulers, against the authorities, against the powers of this dark world and against the spiritual forces of evil in the heavenly realms." Ephesians 6:12. We are at war. Our enemy is deceitful, cunning, and plotting against us. However, 1 John 4:4 tells us, greater is He that is in us than he that is in the world. Our enemy cannot stand against us when we are fully armed by God and implement all the armor and weapons our relationship with Him affords us. "What, then, shall we say in response to these things? If God is for us, who can be against us?" Romans 8:31.

God grants us truth, the truth about Himself, ourselves, those around us, our circumstances, everything. Our relationship with Him is built on truth. It is the belt that holds all else together. Without the truth of God and about God, nothing else given to us to defend us would matter. Nothing else would have any value. If God's Word to us was not true, our faith would be built on sinking sand, and there would be no way to stand firm against the onslaught of Satan's lies. But because God's Word is true, because He is trustworthy, He gives us His Son's righteousness to wear as a breastplate to protect our hearts. We are not righteous on our own, but Jesus chooses to give us His righteousness, His right relationship with God, if we just accept it. This relationship fills the void in our hearts, the void that can only be filled with God's love. Satan tempts us to fill that void with a vast array of temporary fixes, each one leaving us more empty than the one before. God's righteousness protects us from these temptations. The void is filled, and we know that nothing else can satisfy that longing, that void, besides our relationship with God.

God also arms us with the Gospel of peace. The Good News that Jesus paid the price of our sin for us fills us with peace that we do not have to strive to be good enough to earn salvation. It is a gift. Romans 5:1-2 tells us that Jesus taking our place also restores peace between us and God. Because God sees us through the lens of Jesus's righteousness, our relationship with God is no longer broken. It is restored to the friendship we were created to have with Him, thus bringing peace between us. This good news and this peace allow us to dig our feet in and be ready for any attack of the devil to unsettle us, to rattle us, to distract us. The awesome part is, as Priscilla Shirer explains in her "Armor of God" study[11], it not only allows us to dig in, it also allows us to take back ground from Satan that he gains when we allow him to weasel into a chink in our armor. None of us are perfect. We let our guard down occasionally, and Satan pounces. We may get knocked down, but we are not defeated. The grace of the Gospel covers it all, past, present, and future indiscretions. That grace erases any guilt and replaces it with peace, removing that particular weapon from Satan's arsenal and letting us take ground back from him.

God gives us a shield of faith, the ability to act upon our belief and trust in Him. This creates a barrier between us and Satan that prevents his diversionary tactics from getting to us. If he cannot get us to stumble, he will send fiery darts at us triggering a brush fire that we think we need to extinguish, distracting us from what God really needs us to do. Our faith keeps us focused, and our trust in God reminds us to let God handle the fire fights that are not our battles to engage in. Satan loves to shoot darts at us that tempt us to focus on defending ourselves, our calling, our path, or a number of other things, expending time and energy that would be better spent actually doing our calling, fulfilling our purpose, and continuing down the path ahead of us. This was one of his main tactics during World. Praying for God to fight for me in these instances allowed me to remain focused on what He had called me to do: bring Him glory at World.

God also guards our minds with the helmet of salvation. Satan's favorite tactics include putting doubt in our mind about our worth, to ourselves, to God, to others, attacking us with all kinds of lies and self-deprecating thoughts. Our salvation acts as a helmet to protect our mind from such debilitating attacks. If anything could instill worth in ourselves, it is the fact that even if we were the only one who ever disobeyed God, the only one who would ever be eternally separated from God, He would have still sent Jesus to die for us, to be beaten, tortured, condemned, separated from His Father. Just. For. Us. Each one of us is that important to God, that treasured, that cherished, that loved. What we have to offer God and others is that special, that precious, that He redeemed us so that that gift we have to give would not be lost or wasted. He made sure we could be His child, His friend, a part of His plan to save the world. No lie of Satan will ever change any of that. Our salvation sees to that.

The weapons we have been given are the Word of God and prayer. The Bible, the Sword of the Spirit, God's written truth, will defeat any lie, any cunning, deceitful tactic thrown at us. Anytime. Every time. It will pierce through falsehoods and half-truths. It will drive off doubts, fears, and worry. Satan cannot be where God is, for evil cannot be in the presence of a perfect and holy God. Satan can only come near us when we allow him a toe hold, allow him to gain territory into our lives. God's Word and His Spirit keep God's presence with us at all times, readily accessible, driving back Satan and his forces of darkness, as a sword drives back the enemy and keeps him at bay. Prayer brings us into God's presence and allows us to seek His wisdom, His discernment, His guidance in all aspects of our lives, arming us preemptively and in the heat of the battle to combat the tactics of our enemy.

God also gave us each other. Fellow believers. Battle buddies in spiritual warfare. As a soldier never fights alone, neither do soldiers of Christ. We fight in prayer together. Through prayer we call upon the greatest Battle Buddy we could have, God Almighty Himself. In Exodus 14:14, it says, "The LORD will fight for you, you need only to be still." That is why we do not have to worry about those diversionary fire fights. God will fight those for us. He will fight for us, in our place and for our attention and affection. He is a jealous God and will do whatever it takes to keep our eyes focused on Him. He will protect us and fight for us when Satan attacks. He will fight for our attention when we fall for Satan's tactics. He will always provide a way out when we are tempted and attacked. 1 Corinthians 10:13 promises that. "Submit yourselves, then, to God. Resist the devil, and he will flee from you. Come near to God and He will come near to you." James 4:7-8a. God is our greatest ally. With Him at our side, we can resist Satan and send him packing. All God asks is that we put Him first, that we put our relationship with Him first, taking time to get to know Him, His ways, and His expectations for us, and adjusting our lives to suit Him, something we should do willingly after all He has done for us.

We always need to remember that "God is our refuge and strength, an ever-present help in trouble." Psalm 46:1. "The LORD is good, a refuge in times of trouble. He cares for those who trust in him." Nahum 1:7. God protects us by providing us with armor and by fighting for us, but He also protects us by being our safe place to retreat to in order to regroup, renew, and restore our soul before returning to battle. He is always there to help us, strengthen us, tend to our wounds. He knows our limits, and His presence is where we can go in the heat of the battle to rest before returning to the fight.

Sometimes, unfortunately, things get worse before they get better. As I mentioned before, "the darkest hour is just before dawn." In Exodus 5, Moses and Aaron have gone before Pharaoh telling Him to let God's people go. His response: make bricks without straw. A bad situation got worse. It took that, though, for the Israelites to see that they truly needed delivering. That is, after they blamed Moses and Aaron for making their lives worse. In Exodus 6:5-8, God says He heard the groaning of the Israelites, and He will free them from slavery, making them His chosen people, and bring them into the Promised Land. God's response to Pharaoh: plagues. Things got worse for everyone before they finally got better, and the Israelites were freed. The same thing happens in our lives. We are in a difficult situation, and our attempts to improve it seem to make it worse, or it simply gets worse despite our efforts, and it does not improve until God steps in in a mighty way. God allows conditions to deteriorate before He intervenes in order for us to truly see our need for Him, to truly see we cannot rectify the situation on our own, and for His deliverance to be grand and wonderous, a testimony to all of His power and glory.

When God shows up to intervene, more often than not, He chooses an outside of the box method to prove He intervened and not anyone else. Take the Battle of Jericho, for instance, in Joshua 5:13-6:27. There was nothing ordinary about marching around the city everyday and then the wall crumbling at the trumpet blast and the people's shout. Then there is Gideon in Judges 6-7. Because of God, he and 300 men defeated the Midianite army with trumpets, clay jars, and torches. God used the commotion to throw the Midianite army into confusion, and they turned on themselves. Gideon and his men just sat back and watched God fight for them. God will show up and fight for us, too. It will not always happen when and how we think it should, but when God intervenes, He will show up in a mighty way and leave no doubt in our mind or the minds of anyone else involved that it was He who fought on our behalf.

Points to Ponder...

- Looking back, how have you seen God's hand of protection in your life? What has He protected you from, and how is He protecting you now?

- Think about each piece of armor and each weapon God has given you. How are you currently using each one? How can you use each one more effectively?

- What are some outside of the box ways God has intervened in your life? Have you taken time to show your gratitude and share your story with others to encourage them and give God glory?

Chapter 12

Perseverance

"I have fought the good fight, I have finished the race,
I have kept the faith."
2 Timothy 4:7

This journey we are on with God will be absolutely incredible, but it will not be an easy one. Jesus made a point to tell us this so that we would know that having struggles is not unique to us. It is normal, and we are not the only ones facing difficulties in our lives. Life is not singling us out and targeting us with trials. Everyone faces them. He said, "I have told you these things, so that in me you may have peace. In this world you will have trouble. But take heart! I have overcome the world." John 16:33. Knowing we are not alone in our struggles gives us peace and courage, especially when the One by our side is the One who defeated sin and death and faced greater hardship than we could ever imagine. When One who has been through more, through darker, and rose victorious, walks at our side, guiding us, encouraging us, we know we can fully trust Him because He has been in our shoes and understands. This gives us the peace and confidence we need to press on and persevere through the trials that arise from following God's calling on our life.

Aria's and my journey to our World Championship took time, patience, and reliance on God. It required hours upon hours of training, lessons, and dozens of shows to prepare. A year or so prior to taking home our title, I was driving to the barn and thinking about an upcoming show. One thought led to another…how Aria and I seemed to be improving, but how we always tend to show with people better than us. That was when God impressed upon me that it is not that they are "better." They are just further along in their journey. God sets the pace for our journey in life towards our goals and dreams. Some people seem to move at a faster or slower pace than we do towards goals and dreams, and we see them as "better" or "worse" at something that we are, when that is not the case at all. God just picked a different pace for them than He deemed best for us. We all grow and mature at different rates, and He sets the pace for our journey that best suits our most efficient growth rate. We also have to keep in mind we do not all start our journey at the same time. Some begin chasing a dream early in life, some later. Therefore, someone who seems further along than us simply has been growing longer than we have, and someone who does not seem as far along, simply has not been growing as long as we have. We also may not even be headed after the same goal or dream, even if it looks like it from our perspective, and that is why their pace seems so different than ours. God's plan and God's pace for accomplishing His plan are perfect and are unique to each of us. We need to match His pacing rather than try to match the pacing of someone else whose journey is not the same as the one God designed for us. God also puts us at the point we are in our journey to look to those further along for encouragement and inspiration and to offer the same encouragement and inspiration to those who are not as far along as we are. God slowed the pace of Aria's and my journey after World, and I am not sure why though I have no doubt He has allowed this in order to accomplish what is best for us. I must trust His judgement and continue to rely on Him as together we persevere through this time of healing. I am grateful for those God has placed in my life who are further along in their journey than I am in mine. Their encouragement and wisdom have been invaluable during this time, and my prayer is that those who are not as far along as Aria and I will find hope and inspiration from how God is working in our journey.

Sometimes, unfortunately, the difficulties we face are of our own making. Even when we strive to follow God's plan, we can get distracted, mistaking our will for His, and march off down a path not of His design, a path that leads to heartache and despair because it is outside of His will. Other times, we stumble. We give in to temptation. We get caught up in a fire fight we are not supposed to engage in. We willfully disobey God because we get tired of waiting on His plan, so we run ahead and try to force His will to happen on our time table rather than His, which makes a mess of things. This again puts us on a path of hardship that is not part of God's plan but He allows anyways because He knows we must endure the consequences of the path we chose before we can see our error and our need to repent and get back on the right path. That moment we realize our mistake, we have a tendency to feel like we have completely blown it, and God will be so disappointed in us He will reject us and refuse to use us in His service. That could not be any further from the truth. "No, in all these things we are more than conquerors through him who loved us. For I am convinced that neither death nor life, neither angels nor demons, neither the present nor the future, nor any powers, neither height nor depth, nor anything else in all creation, will be able to separate us from the love of God that is in Christ Jesus our Lord." Romans 8:37-39. No matter what we have done, no matter what we struggle with, God will always love us, and through Jesus we can conquer anything.

That does not necessarily mean that we can always conquer it just us and God, especially when dealing with struggles like addiction, trauma, depression, and long-term, unhealthy patterns of behavior. This does mean that God will lead us to the right people to help us conquer our struggle when we realize it is bigger than we can handle on our own, even with God at our side, and we reach out for help. The very people He sends to help us are most likely the very ones who, at some point in their life, stood in our shoes battling the very same things, and through God's grace, persevered. They are living proof that NOTHING can separate us from God's love, and NOTHING makes us so broken that God cannot still use us. They will use their experience, what worked for them and what did not in their battle, to guide us in our battle. The very thing that we thought would make us unusable is the very thing that makes them fully capable to minister as God has called them. That gives us great hope when all feels lost. "Praise be to the God and Father of our Lord Jesus Christ, the Father of compassion and the God of all comfort, who comforts us in all our troubles, so that we can comfort those in any trouble with the comfort we ourselves have received from God." 2 Corinthians 1:3-4. The comfort and compassion God provided them in their battle, they pass on to us in ours, and in time, we too may pass it on to someone else in theirs.

Remember, God promises in Romans 8:28 that He can and will use all things for good for those that love Him and are called according to His purpose. That means He already has a plan on how to use any stumble of ours for good down the road. It could very well be that one day we are the one answering someone else's cry for help, and we can draw upon our own experience, including what we learn from those God placed in our life when we needed help. The mentored becomes the mentor. Never forget that God loves to use broken people. "But we have this treasure in jars of clay to show that this all-surpassing power is from God and not from us. We are hard pressed on every side, but not crushed; perplexed but not in despair; persecuted, but not abandoned; struck down but not destroyed." 2 Corinthians 4:7-9. Broken people let God's light shine through the cracks. We walk away from what tried to destroy us with an awesome testimony of how God sustained us and rescued us. Our perseverance through God's sustaining power might be just what inspires someone else to take that first step towards relying on God. If just one soul comes to Christ because of all we have endured, then it is all worth it.

It is very possible that one day, Aria and I will be the ones offering encouragement to someone going through a similar situation as ours. Maybe one day I will use the lessons we learned through this journey from World Champions to sidelined by injury to being used again in some capacity by God to help some other rider with an injured horse, or some individual with an injury of body, mind, or spirit. Maybe I already am. Maybe as you read this you are starting to realize that even though you feel broken, you are not forgotten by God. You are still useable and still being used and will still be used by God in some inspiring capacity that is beyond your wildest imaginings at this moment. Maybe, just maybe, you will be inspired by our story to continue on and persevere in yours.

When we are at our weakest, when we are our most vulnerable, that is when God's power shines through the most. "But he said to me, 'My grace is sufficient for you, for my power is made perfect in weakness." 2 Corinthians 12:9. No matter the cause of what we face, whether of our own making or not, we can persevere because of God's strength. "I know what it is to be in need, and I know what it is to have plenty. I have learned the secret of being content in any and every situation, whether well fed or hungry, whether living in plenty or in want. I can do everything though him who gives me strength." Philippians 4:12-13. The key to peace and contentment and the ability to persevere in any situation we face, good or bad, divinely orchestrated or of our own making, is to trust God and lean on His strength rather than our own. There is nothing that we face that He does not already have a plan to handle.

If He has brought us to it, or allowed us to be brought to it, He will see us through it. 1 Peter 5:7 says, "Cast all your anxiety on him because he cares for you." All our cares. All our anxieties. All that troubles us. He wants us to bring them all to Him, to discuss them, for Him to offer guidance on what we should do and what we should leave for Him to do.

God never wants us to go it alone. He never wants us to think, "I got myself into this mess. Now I have got to get myself out of it." Proverbs 3:5-6 tells us God does not want us to trust our own understanding or rely on ourselves to fix things or figure things out. He wants us to trust Him with every fiber of our being, acknowledge Him in all we say and do, look to Him for guidance, and He will make the path clear to us. Even if we feel like we have wandered a million miles away from the path God put us on originally, He will still guide us back. "[B]eing confident of this, that he who began a good work in you will carry it on to completion until the day of Christ Jesus." Philippians 1:6. What God started in us, He will finish. He will not leave us hanging, and He will not hang us out to dry no matter how many bumps in the road. No matter how many setbacks in Aria's healing process we faced, this verse gave me hope that God would finish what He started in us. He started the good work of Aria's healing, so He would see it through. He started using us as instrument to testify of His goodness and grace, so He would continue to demonstrate those characteristics in our lives. We would be, and are, examples of how He purposefully uses those who have been broken and scarred, "so that people may see and know, may consider and understand, that the hand of the LORD has done this" Isaiah 41:20.

Philippians 1:6 is also of great comfort in times when God is silent. Those times when it feels like God has stopped moving or stopped speaking. We pour over everything we have said and done that could have possibly caused Him to take a step back. We repent of all we can think of. We have let the Holy Spirit mold our heart and character to conform them to His, and yet, God is still silent. Take heart. There is a reason for the delay. God will finish what He started. He will bring about the vision He gave you. He will open the doors needed for you to fulfill His calling on your life. The delay has a purpose. It teaches us to trust Him even when life does not make sense. It helps us grow and mature in Him, so we can more fully appreciate when He does move and opens doors for us.

Sometimes the delay is not because of us but because of some other party that is an integral part of His plan for us. It could be the position He has lined up for you simply is not available yet because the person currently holding it has not yet seen the new opportunity God is calling them to. It could be that your dream home is not on the market yet because the family living there still has one child to send off to college before they will downsize. It could be that the man or woman of your dreams has pressing matters God needs them to attend to before their heart is ready for a relationship with you. The list goes on and on. All we can do is make sure our heart is right with God, that we are truly focused on what He wants and not on what we want, so that we are ready when He does move, and we are not willfully the cause of God's delay in our own life or someone else's life. God may not be able to open the doors someone else needs opened until we are ready for our part in God's plan for them, whatever it may be.

We are all pieces on a chess board that only God can see. He sees how all the pieces are arranged on the board and knows the best order to move the pieces so that His great, overreaching plan is accomplished. Any chess player knows, pieces must be moved methodically and strategically. Just because our piece is not moving does not mean the game is over. God is moving other pieces that we cannot see that are necessary to be in place before it is our turn to move. We have to trust that God knows best when to move which piece simply because He can see the whole board, and we can only see the few pieces around us. God does see you and your situation, and He in time will move and use it for good and for His glory. Just like the rejected stone becomes the capstone Jesus referred to in Matthew 21:42, just because we feel overlooked or unusable does not mean God has overlooked us.

I may never know exactly why God allowed Aria to be injured after World, causing us to be sidelined as she healed. I do not know what all is going on in the background that I cannot see that needs to be in place before God is ready to use us in a more active role. I do, however, know that His timing in Aria's recovery is perfect, from the timing of our picture being hung in town on Momma's birthday to the timing of when we were cleared to ride at the walk. This came between the one-year anniversary of Momma's passing and of her funeral. That was an incredibly difficult, emotional week, feeling sadness due to missing Momma terribly but also peace knowing that she is fully restored and living in the presence of God, singing praises to the King. When I got the message suggesting I ride Aria at the walk to see how she was doing, it was as if a beam of joy pierced through the darkness of my heart. When I carefully got on her that evening, and we took those first tentative steps, tears of happiness welled up in my eyes as she felt as good and as sound as she did before the injury. God knew exactly what I needed that week to persevere, to renew my hope that He will, in fact, continue to restore Aria to complete soundness, bringing light to an otherwise dark week. It was His, and Momma's, way of reminding me that there is joy in life still, and that He sees us. Even though our chess piece is not making many moves on the chess board of life at the moment, that one move reminded me that the game is still in play. When the time is right, He will move us again, progressing from just walking to trotting when Aria shows she is ready, and eventually to cantering. One day at a time, in God's perfect timing, we will persevere through this wilderness.

These times of delay are times to stop and wait on God. Do not try to rush ahead and force God's will to happen even if you think you know what is supposed to happen next. Doing so just makes a mess of things and may inadvertently make the delay longer as God has to repair the damage done by plowing ahead without Him. If we rushed Aria's recovery, pushing her faster than her leg was ready to handle, we could not only reinjure her leg, delaying healing even more, but might also do severe damage that would cause her to never be fully sound. All because we wanted things on our timetable instead of God's. It is much better to wait on Him, be patient, and trust His timetable for her recovery is best. Isaiah 40:28-31 says, "Do you not know? Have you not heard? The LORD is the everlasting God, the Creator of the ends of the earth. He will not grow tired or weary, and his understanding no one can fathom. He gives strength to the weary and increases the power of the weak. Even youths grow tired and weary, and young men stumble and fall; but those that hope in [or "wait upon" in KJV] the LORD will renew their strength. They will soar on wings like eagles; they will run and not grow weary, they will walk and not be faint." Times of delay can be times of renewal if we allow them to be. Waiting on God, spending time in His presence, putting our hope and trust in Him, can and will deepen our relationship with Him, taking our intimacy with Him to a deeper level, giving us a greater understanding of God's mind and heart. Then, when He does move, we are so in tune with Him that following Him and discerning His will is as natural as breathing.

"Delight yourself in the LORD and he will give you the desires of your heart. Commit your way to the LORD; trust in him and he will do this: He will make your righteousness shine like the dawn, the justice of your cause like the noonday sun. Be still before the LORD and wait patiently for him; do not fret when men succeed in their ways, when they carry out their wicked schemes." Psalm 37:4-7. It is very disheartening when we are doing all we can to follow God and to stay in line with His will, and yet God has us in a time of waiting while others who are blatantly serving themselves obtain the very things we are waiting for God to provide. While this has not happened in regards to Aria's healing, it has at times in other areas of my life. I have wondered why them and not me? Or why me and not them? When we put God first, though, when we wait on Him and take delight in Him, when we persevere through a time of delay, and God starts opening doors in a mighty way, He will do so in a way that will not only bring Him glory, but also will allow others to see how our heart stayed true to Him through the emotional ups and downs of delay. We must always remember it is not a matter of IF God will show up in our circumstances, but WHEN, and when He shows up will be at the perfect time to make the greatest impact in our lives and in the lives of those in our circle of influence. His providence and our perseverance will give hope to others struggling in darkness, waiting on God to move, searching for a reason, a source of hope.

This is what happened in 2 Chronicles 15 during Asa's reign as king of Judah. The chapter opens with Azariah prophesying to Asa and all of Judah and Benjamin. In verse 2, he says, "The LORD is with you when you are with him. If you seek him, he will be found by you, but if you forsake him, he will forsake you." To illustrate his point, he told of how Israel had turned from God and how they had gone a long time without His Word and without priests to teach them His ways. God allowed them to be oppressed to remind them of their need for Him. "But in their distress they turned to the LORD, the God of Israel, and sought him, and he was found by them." 2 Chronicles 15:4. "But as for you, [Asa,] be strong and do not give up, for your work will be rewarded." Verse 7. If God could be found by Israel after they had forsaken Him for so long, then since Asa was striving to do "what was good and right in the eyes of the LORD his God," according to 2 Chronicles 14:2, God would surely reward his efforts if Asa persevered in leading Judah to follow in God's ways. His steadfastness to God, and God's steadfastness to Asa brought hope to the people during troublesome times. 2 Chronicles 15:9b says "large numbers had come over to him from Israel when they saw that the LORD his God was with him." Asa assembled the people, and they as a nation took an oath to seek God and His will with all their heart and soul and always put Him first. "All Judah rejoiced about the oath because they had sworn it wholeheartedly. They sought God eagerly, and he was found by them. So the LORD gave them rest on every side." Verse 15. God rewarded Asa's work of putting God first, and leading the nation to do the same, with peace. Others saw what God was doing in Judah, and they wanted to be a part of it. They wanted that same peace, that same rest, that same protection Judah had, and they could not get it any other way but through seeking God. When we are in distress, God will reward our efforts if we remain strong and persevere, keeping Him and His Word first and foremost in our lives. He will give us the rest and peace that comes from His presence, just like He gave Judah. Our steadfastness to God and His steadfastness to us will draw others to Him. They will see the good that God works through us and our circumstances. They will see the benefits of having a right relationship with God, and they will want that for themselves, not just because of what God can do for them, but also because of what He has already done for them through Christ.

"The people walking in darkness have seen a great light; on those living in the land of the shadow of death a light has dawned." Isaiah 9:2. That light is Christ, and we are the vessel He uses to shine into the darkness to be a beacon to draw people to Him. You are a beacon His light shines through. His presence in you. Your perspective on life. Your time spent preparing for your unique purpose. God's provision and protection. The strength afforded to you to persevere and pursue His calling on your life. All of that enables God to use you to shine His light into the darkness, give hope to the hopeless, peace to the despairing. You are the only Jesus so many will see. Reflect Him well. Use the testimony of His presence in your life to show them His presence in their life. Show them the grace made available to them by Jesus. Do all this using the unique gifts and talents God has given you. Let it be said of you, "I have fought the good fight, I have finished the race, I have kept the faith." 2 Timothy 4:7.

As the writer said in Hebrews 13:20-21, "May the God of peace, who through the blood of the eternal covenant brought back from the dead our Lord Jesus, that great Shepherd of the sheep, equip you with everything good for doing his will, and may he work in us what is pleasing to him through Jesus Christ, to whom be glory for ever and ever. Amen."

Points to Ponder...

- How has God encouraged you to persevere in your current circumstances or in your latest difficulty if you are in a time of peace?
- How have you had to trust God's timing and wait on Him to move?
- How has God equipped you to help others with their struggles? What brokenness and scars do you have that God can let His light shine through?

My Plan   *God's Plan*

Promised Land

Promised Land

Jordan River

Red Sea

Wilderness

Red Sea

The Jordan River

"being confident of this, that he who began a good work in you will carry it on to completion until the day of Christ Jesus."

Philippians 1:6

Chapter 13

Pressing On

"We walk by faith, not by sight."
2 Corinthians 5:7 (NKJV)

As Aria's leg healed, we slowly increased how much rehab I did with her. It was time to put all the lessons God had been impressing upon me into action. Our trek in the wilderness was beginning to approach the Jordan River, a moment of stepping out in faith, trusting His promises rather than fearing the giants of uncertainty in the land ahead. At first, I only worked with her on the ground, and then once cleared to ride her at the walk, I gradually increased the duration of our rides, building stamina and also allowing her to learn to trust her leg again. This slow pace gave us the opportunity to fill in "holes" in our training, things like learning to pivot correctly around her inside hind foot and developing a truly extended walk with a bigger stride and faster pace than her ordinary walk, things that had been our weaknesses that we now had time to polish and turn into strengths. Sometimes God slows the pace in our lives so that we too can work on weaknesses that we had been putting off dealing with for one reason or another. Adequately addressing these weaknesses make us stronger, more capable, when God returns us to "active duty," just like if Aria and I were to return to the show pen, addressing our weaknesses during this time in the wilderness will improve our performances, and thus our scores, and maybe even our placings. I realized God had purposefully slowed the pace of my life so that I could truly heal from all the hurt and brokenness that transpired around Momma's passing and the spiritual warfare in the months that followed. It was not just Aria that needed to heal. My heart needed to heal as well before God could truly use me again in His service. Our time in the wilderness gave me that opportunity. Like Aria, I may still have scars, but God will use those scars to minister to others in ways that would have been impossible beforehand. God was showing me the good He was bringing about from the bad.

One of my biggest fears through Aria's healing process was if she would feel the same once the scar tissue was set. Her gaits have always been silky smooth. That is what makes her such a comfortable ride. God gave me much needed hope when she felt the same at the walk, but the true test would be when we were cleared to trot. The trot, while the most efficient of all the gaits, it also has the most concussion, which is why it is the gait used to detect lameness. Any pain or restriction in movement will show up when trotting. About six weeks after we began our walk rides, the vet gave us the nod to see how well Aria would handle trotting. That evening our ride began like any other. Shorty was running around chasing grasshoppers as Aria and I walked around the pen, first her ordinary walk and then her extended walk. I took a deep breath, said a prayer asking for a miracle, and squeezed Aria up into the trot. At first, she hesitated. Up until this point, every time she attempted to trot, I would correct her and bring her back down to the walk. When she realized this time I actually wanted her to trot, I felt her relax and step into it confidently. My plan had been to just slowly jog around the pen, but she was so happy to get to trot she stretched out her stride to moderate pace, practically floating around the paddock. I nearly cried. I would have, but Shorty was so happy about her trotting, too, that he was literally running circles around us, and I had to keep my eyes open so that I could keep us from colliding should there be any close calls. God had done it again. He had fought for us, and though her leg still did not look normal, through His miraculous, mighty, healing hand, Aria *felt* perfectly normal. In that moment, I knew beyond a shadow of a doubt, even if her leg is scarred, she and I will still be perfectly usable by God. As Matthew West sings in "Broken Things," "But if it's true You use broken things, Then here I am, Lord, I'm all Yours. The pages of history they tell me it's true That it's never the perfect; it's always the ones with the scars that You use." [12] That song has resonated with me throughout Aria's healing process. God may still fully restore the appearance of her leg, only time will tell on that, but if not, that is okay, too. We are still usable by Him either way. Through this, He gave me the assurance that we were nearing the end of our time in the wilderness and approaching the Promised Land He has for us.

What that Promised Land is remained to be seen, but I was now brave enough to dream of it. Our toes were at the edge of the

Jordan, and I dared to peer across to see what might lie ahead for us. It all rested on how well she rehabbed and how much of a work load she can handle. If she continued to do well, even once we were cleared to canter, we would then see how she handled working in a sand arena. If that went well, we might be able to lightly show, each class being an opportunity to testify to the greatness of God and His grace allowing us to return to the show ring after her injury. Even if she could not show again, she would still be a perfect example of how God through His grace binds what is broken in us and restores us and our relationship to Him when we stumble, and how He is still willing to use us, scars and all, to point others to Him. My prayer is He will use our story to encourage others, to encourage you, that if He will lead us through the wilderness and into the Promised Land in our lives, He will do the same for you in your life. Whatever wilderness you are in now, it will not last forever. You will grow. You will heal. You may have scars from the experience, but those scars will not keep you from being used by God. He will use you because of your scars. The story your scars tell will be the perfect platform for you to tell of God's healing in your own life and in your own heart and of how you grew spiritually, emotionally, even physically, because God slowed the pace of your journey down and caused you to spend some time in the wilderness, just like He did in my life. You too will enter into whatever Promised Land God has in store for you, and it will be greater than anything you can imagine! Just keep trusting Him. Just keep following Him. Just keep listening to Him.

I will admit I wrestled with fear and insecurity as we drew closer to leaving the wilderness of Aria's healing process. There is security and comfort in the routine of regular vet trips and the limitations to our rides, especially compared to the uncertainty of what may happen when we start seeing the vet less frequently, as well as what may happen when we attempt cantering and riding on arena footing. There was nagging fear of reinjury and that it would be my fault. Those were the moments I saw the size of the "giants in the land" rather than the size of the God Who has brought us to this point in our journey. These were also the moments God reminded me of His promises of His presence, provision, and protection. He had brought us this far. He would not abandon us now. He would continue the good work He started in us and see it to completion. The "giants" that lay ahead of us would be no match for the mighty God we serve.

Aria's attitude brightened immensely since starting back to work. She loves to have a "job," a sense of purpose. Boredom does not suit her, and being laid up made her rather depressed. Joy returned to her eyes when she realized she still had a job to do. This caused me to entertain the idea of setting a goal of attending a show, the Margarita Classic in Waco, in late fall, over a year after her initial injury, about ten months after the second, more devastating one, and about five months since we started rehabilitation, rather than waiting until spring. This was partially due to concern of reinjury during the winter, since our winters tend to be wet and muddy, factors that contributed to her injury in the first place. My thoughts were that if she handled cantering as well as she handled trotting, and if she handled arena footing well, especially with support wraps, then she should be able to participate in amateur SPB hunt seat equitation by then. Since she has gone through so much, I only wanted to show in one class our first time back so that I did not ask too much of her too soon. In the back of my mind, I had been toying with the goal of earning what is called a "Register of Merit," or "ROM," in this particular class as well. Placing well in an APHA class earns points, and ten are required to earn an ROM in that class. Due to 2017 World and previous shows, we had earned eight points in amateur SPB hunt seat equitation, leaving us only needing two for our ROM, an attainable goal if God was in it. We were once again in the position of doing our part and giving our best effort, leaving the results in God's most capable hands. All I could do was be very in tune with Aria as I ride, feeling every step, every movement, to ensure I was not asking her to do anything that made her uncomfortable, only asking for more from her as she gained strength and confidence. Then I had to trust the Still, Small Voice of the Holy Spirit as to when it was time to step out of the wilderness and back into the show ring, if that was God's will for us and part of the Promised Land He has in store for us.

Nearly two months after we began trotting, we were cleared to continue to gradually increase Aria's exercise as she could tolerate it. When I tacked her up for the first time since World, I could sense Aria was excited but guarded about what was to come. Because of the heat and because I wanted to feel exactly how Aria was moving, up to this point, I had only ridden bareback. We walked around for a while just so she could relax and for us to both take in the moment. Just sitting on her in English tack was an answer to prayer. What lay ahead in our ride would reveal how God answered more prayers. As I asked her for the posting trot, which was just a bit more forward than what we had been trotting, she still felt guarded. I knew she had to learn to trust her leg again, so I reassured her as best I could. Before long, I felt her relax again. After repeating the process the other direction, I said a quick prayer and squeezed her up into the canter. She struck off instantly, her joy being expressed with a playful head toss as she cantered around the pen. Shorty was so excited he had to run alongside us looking up at his big sister with pure bliss on his face. Her confidence grew with each stride, and when we cantered the other direction, she felt wonderful. At all gaits under tack, she carried herself in a beautiful frame, relaxed head carriage, soft expression. God had shown up for us yet again and blessed us abundantly. While, as of yet, Aria's leg still remains larger than her other front leg, God has restored her and healed her body so that she moves well and feels as smooth as before her injury. The next time we rode tacked up, Aria moved confidently at all gaits, no hesitation or guardedness. Her transitions were effortless, light and precise, as if we had not missed a day of training, rather than it being nearly a year since we had worked under saddle. Words cannot adequately express just how overwhelmed I was in that moment by God's goodness and graciousness.

The show I had set as our "comeback" goal was still a few months out. I knew I needed to spend that time listening for that Still, Small Voice for guidance, as well as continue to "listen" to Aria as we worked to get back into shape. If Aria continued to rehabilitate well, and we were ready to show by then, that was great. If she needed more time, then that was perfectly alright as well. Both God and Aria would make it clear what to do as the show approached.

Nearly a month after we introduced cantering to our rehab rides, we reached another milestone. I scheduled a lesson with Tracey so that we could evaluate not only how well she handled arena footing, but primarily to see if she truly was doing as well as she felt. I did not want to get my hopes up and start dreaming of a comeback show and getting our Register of Merit before getting Tracey's opinion on Aria's soundness and potential. That morning I had mixed emotions, excitement, but also fear. I realized that must have been exactly how the Israelites felt standing at the edge of the wilderness, on the banks of the Jordan, looking out at the yet unknown Promised Land. There is comfort in the familiarity of the wilderness, uncertainty and insecurity in stepping out into the unknown, and fear of failure, but also excitement knowing that if God is in it, it will be greater than anything imaginable. My main concern was that I wanted to continue to match pace with God, neither lagging behind in the wilderness of healing nor forging ahead of Him, risking injury to Aria. As we were loading up, I received a text of Psalm 56:3, "When I am afraid, I will trust in you." It was God's way of reminding me to trust Him. He had brought us to that moment, to the edge of our wilderness and on the brink of our Promised Land. It was time to trust Him.

When we arrived, Aria knew exactly where she was and was excited, not anxious, just ready to go. Tracey and Kayla both checked out Aria's leg and commented on how much it had improved. I mounted up, and Aria and I set off at a walk. She was more than willing to extend her walk into a forward, free swinging step. After walking for some time to loosen up, Tracey asked us to trot and watched us carefully. While Aria was putting full weight on her recovering leg, the scar tissue naturally prohibited her leg from moving exactly like her other front leg, causing a slight mechanical difference and a bit shorter stride, not enough for her to appear lame and possibly not even noticeable unless you were specifically looking for it. After another walk break, Tracey had us canter. I nearly cried when she said it was absolutely lovely. I fought back tears as we finished up and discussed the possibility of going for our ROM. God has been so gracious. When she first tore her tendon, I had no idea if I would ever ride her again. Now we are a walking, trotting, cantering testimony of the power of God, of prayer, of hard work, and of following the vet's instructions. Now we were not only riding, but pending vet approval, talking about getting her back in shape and doing a comeback show. God has shown up for us again in a mighty way. I do not know what the future holds for us still, but I know Who holds the future, and I know that the present constitutes a miracle.

Points to Ponder...

- Where are you at in your wilderness experience? How have you seen God use it to transform you as you have walked with Him through it?

- What hints has God been giving you that you may be approaching your Jordan River? If you are still deep in the wilderness, what signs has God impressed on you to look for to know your wilderness time is ending?

- What giants do you see up ahead? How is God bigger than them? How will He slay them?

Chapter 14

Parting Waters

"Joshua told the people, 'Consecrate yourselves for tomorrow the LORD will do amazing things among you…And as soon as the priests who carry the ark of the LORD – the LORD of all the earth – set foot in the Jordan, its waters flowing down stream will be cut off and stand in a heap.'"
Joshua 3:5, 13

At our next vet appointment, we were cleared to gradually get Aria back in shape, and if she was able to get into shape in time, and if she continued to handle the increased amount of exercise, they saw no problem in going to the Margarita Classic that November. However, then it started raining. Not just a day or two of rain, but a couple of weeks of rain with some rounds of very heavy rainfall and only occasional breaks in the weather. Even when it was not raining, water was running through Aria's pen. Riding was not an option, and neither was hauling out to ride elsewhere because we would get stuck if we tried. Thoughts of showing were put on the back burner, and my primary concern was Aria staying safe in the mud. My prayers became, not only for continued healing, but also for God's continued protection. If we did not have time to get ready for the show, that would be okay. Aria is more important than any show, any number of points, any award. There will always be more shows. God always has a reason for delay.

As the show approached, God provided just enough break in the weather that we could safely condition, to a certain extent, and even practice the pattern that was posted in advance. We were not nearly as fit as we had been going into World, but Aria felt comfortable and confident, happy to be back to work. A woman had agreed to show with me in exchange for me showing with her in a class, but at the last minute she backed out of going. We loaded up and hauled out to Waco anyways, trusting that if God wanted our class to be pointed, He could provide another horse and rider for the class. However, as the day of the show progressed, it was clear that this was not His plan. At first, I was disappointed that I was the only rider in the class, but then God impressed upon me that He had orchestrated it this way so that I could focus entirely on the enormity of the moment. We were going back into the show ring after a devastating injury. God had again moved in a mighty way, bringing restoration and healing in a way only He could. That class was as much about Him and about giving Him glory as our classes at World had been. We would not earn an ROM that day, but that was okay. We were there to show once again what God can do. He can take a small-town girl and her horse and make them World Champions. He can take a horrible injury and use it to show His restorative and healing power. He can take whatever mess we have in our lives and use it to create something beautiful, something that brings Him honor and glory.

We took Shorty with us, and it seemed like his presence had a calming effect on Aria in the barn. She was the most relaxed in her stall than I had ever seen her. Normally she would pace and fret, but this time, she just stood around munching hay. We had Shorty secured to the corner of the stall with a cable. This allowed him some freedom but also kept him from going visiting. Shorty seemed to know exactly what he needed to do to help Aria emotionally. He would lay in the aisle just far enough from the stall that he and Aria could see each other. She could relax knowing he was watching out for her, and for us. We would put Shorty back in the truck while we were away from the stall, such as when Aria and I practiced and while we were competing. He was not thrilled to be left in the truck, but he was good about it and was always thrilled when we would all reunite back at the stall afterwards. For his first horse show, Shorty did great. He never bothered any of the other horses around, greeted other dogs like long lost friends, and he generally just watched people as they passed by us. Only a couple of times did he ever bark at anyone. He earned his right to be a horse show dog should we be able to show more in the future.

Emotions were high as Aria and I stepped into the arena for our class. Aria listened to me attentively and laid down a beautiful pattern. It was not perfect, but that was alright. God does not ask for perfection, just our best effort for Him, which is exactly what we tried to do. I choked up as we finished, the weight of the moment sinking in. God had shown up for us yet again. When we got back to the stall, my first thought was that I needed to call Momma and let her know how the class went. Tears welled up as I realized she had been watching us just like she had been at World. She would always be watching over us. At that moment I understood exactly why God wanted me to show alone that first show back. I needed to feel every emotion, process each moment, and not let any of it get swallowed up by competitiveness. There would be shows in the spring to attend to attempt to complete our ROM if we faired the winter well and came out sound. This one had been for us and us alone, to give God honor and glory, to remember why we ride in the first place. We ride for Him and because of Him. Without Him, none of this would have been possible.

With the increased work, Aria's leg has continued to reduce gradually in size, and Dr. Tolle began to transition us from acute levels of laser therapy treatment to maintenance levels, meaning going from treatments multiple times a week, to once a week, to every other week, with the goal being only once a month. Because the fall and winter were so wet, and the resulting mud caused soreness, we sometimes had to return more frequently than originally planned. I would have loved for Aria's healing process to be constant improvement, but unfortunately, it was more two steps forward, one step back. As we approached the one-year marker for her severe tendon injury, Aria developed sesamoiditis in her right front leg, making her then sore in both front legs, due to all the mud and having to compensate to stay safe. At that moment, I felt like I was right back where I was a year before, worried, scared, uncertain as to what God had in mind for us. Dreams of getting our ROM seemed to be potentially unattainable. I again wondered how in the world we would be able to point people to Him if Aria kept getting injured. Then slowly God impressed upon me that our calling is not to pursue points but to pursue Him. He may lead us back into the show ring to serve Him, and He may not. He may have other plans for us, other ways for us to serve Him, during this continued time of healing and following it. Whether we go back into the show ring or not, our purpose is to use our testimony of how God has worked in our lives to point people to Him and encourage other believers in their walk with Him. He was again telling me to trust Him and leave the future in His more than capable hands. My focus needed to be on providing the best care possible for Aria and loving her unconditionally. Just take it one day at a time, making the most of each day, and He would reveal His plan one step at a time. Just because we were still in the wilderness did not mean that the Promised Land for us had vanished. God was just taking longer than I had hoped to lead us into it. I needed to trust His timing rather than my own.

Weeks passed, and Aria slowly began to improve. We made changes to how she was shod in order to relieve pressure on her scarred tendon and on her joints. Shows came and went with us unable to attend, but I was alright with that. Aria's health and soundness would always come first. I knew God was leading, and I needed to simply listen to His guidance and follow. He was working behind the scenes, unseen, like when He heaped up the waters well out of sight of the Israelites and where they were to cross the Jordan in Joshua 3. Even though they could not see how He was orchestrating things in their favor, they still stepped out in faith, and at that moment, His work became evident to all, and they crossed the Jordan on dry ground. I realized the priests had to step out in the water FIRST before they saw how God had been working behind the scenes and before the miracle could happen. I had to continue walking in faith, trusting that God was still working, still orchestrating all things in our favor, and that His handiwork would be made plain at the perfect time. I had to step out in faith first, in complete trust, and then what God was doing for us would be plain for all to see.

Little by little Aria became more fit, walking, trotting, and cantering well. By the end of spring, I decided to take her to a nearby ranch show just to see how she fared. I figured that would be a good litmus test on her soundness as well as her capabilities after all she had been through. Our first attempt in May, it came a flood, and there was no way we could get out with the trailer to make it to the show. After that, there was only one more local show in June before the summer break, so I made plans to attend. The night before the show, the hosting ranch received several inches of rain, but we got barely a sprinkling. Had we gotten as much rain as they had, there would have been no way we could have made that show either. However, God made sure we were able to attend. God had literally parted the waters in a heap so that the rain stayed away from us allowing us to haul out on dry ground. The similarities were uncanny. He clearly wanted us there for a reason. While Aria did not score as well as she did before her injury, which was to be expected, she successfully completed her ranch pleasure classes, and much to my surprise, picking up a half point in amateur and a point in open. Everyone at the show was so encouraging, and that alone was a good reason to be there. God knew just how much I needed the reassurance that we truly were walking out of the wilderness after all this time. The points were just an added bonus. It finally felt like we were starting to cross our Jordan River.

Points to Ponder…

- How is God calling you to step out in faith? What water is He asking you to wade out into before the water parts?

- How has your wilderness experience differed from how you expected it to go? As you approach your Jordan, how is God showing you why that was?

- How do you feel God will use this for good? What do you think your Promised Land will entail?

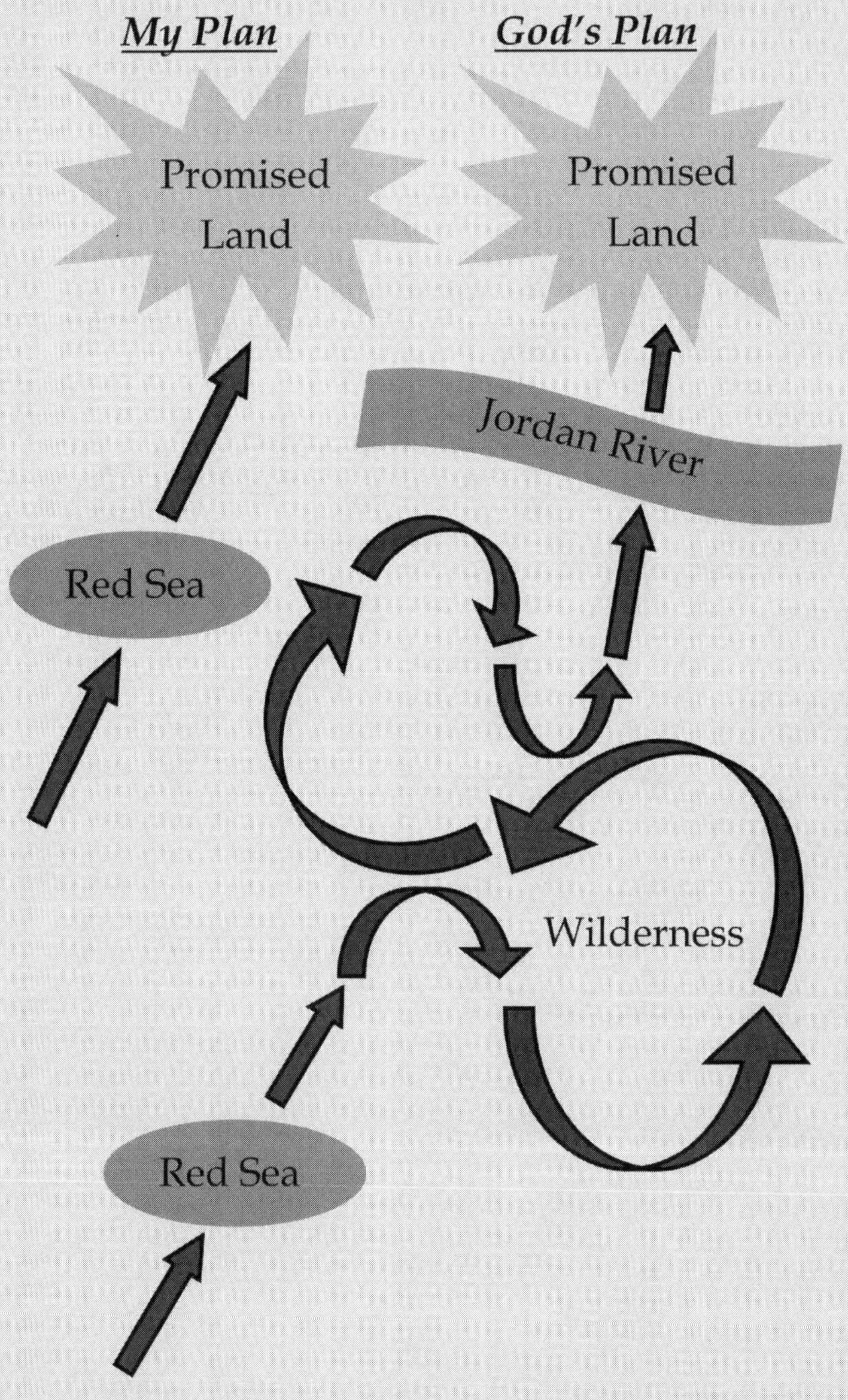
My Plan
God's Plan
Promised Land
Promised Land
Jordan River
Red Sea
Wilderness
Red Sea

The Promised Land

"Jesus looked at them and said, 'With man, this is impossible,

but with God, all things are possible.'"

Matthew 19:26

Chapter 15

"As for me and my horse, will serve the LORD."

"...choose for yourselves this day whom you will serve..."
Joshua 24:15

There was more to God's orchestration in us making that June show than just encouragement though. That show was not just the last one before the break, it was also the last one of the qualifying period for 2019 APHA World. In fact, it was next to the last DAY of the qualifying period. After 2017 World, I really had not even considered going back to World, and then after Aria's injury, it seemed completely impossible. "Jesus looked at them and said, 'With man this is impossible, but with God all things are possible.'" Matthew 19:26. The more I thought on it, the more I saw God's orchestration pointing us back to World. After stepping out in faith and going to the June show, God started showing me how He had been working behind the scenes. The pieces started falling into place. If we had gotten all the points we needed for our ROM at 2017 World, I would have most likely have retired Aria from showing right then. Not having them gave us a goal to work towards during her rehab. If we had gotten our points at the Margarita Classic in 2018, again, there would have been no reason to continue to show. We were unable to make any of the other shows that offered hunt seat equitation, but God went above and beyond to ensure we made that ranch show, finishing our qualification requirements. Those requirements themselves showed His hand in our journey as well. When we first started showing at APHA shows, you had to attend four shows and show before eight judges (typically two or more judges are at each show) in order to qualify for World. However, after 2017 World, around the time of Aria's initial injury, the requirements were changed to just two shows. If they had remained at four shows, there would have been no way we could have qualified for 2019 World. Once again, God had been working behind the scenes on our behalf.

Throughout Aria's healing process, God had impressed upon me over and over that He would receive more glory through her injury and because of her injury than He would have from our 2017 performances alone. Returning to World after all she had been through would be an amazing testimony of what God has done for us, but I wanted to make sure I was hearing God correctly, not just hearing what I wanted to hear or seeing what I wanted to see. I felt more like Gideon than Joshua. I sought affirmation.

First came a sermon on 2 Chronicles 20, where Jehoshaphat received word that three armies were approaching to attack Judah. The preacher spoke about how the king feeling completely overwhelmed, but he found peace when Jahaziel encouraged him in verses 15 through 17, verses that practically leapt off the page at me, reminding him the battle belonged to the Lord, and He would fight the armies for them. In classic, outside-of-the-box style, God set ambushes against the army and defeated them while the men of Judah sang God's praises. The preacher stressed that the battles in our lives are not ours, but God's, that He will fight for us, and we need to leave the results to Him. This instantly reminded me of my constant prayer for 2017 World, that God would go before us and fight for us, as well as Aria's stall sign bearing witness that, while we train and prepare, victory rests with God. If we were to go back to World, it would only be possible "'Not by might nor by power, but by my Spirit,' says the LORD Almighty." Zechariah 4:6. This time around there was no way I could afford lessons, so it would be evident to all that however we did would be solely because of God's greatness. God also reminded me "being confident of this, that he who began a good work in you will carry it on to completion until the day of Christ Jesus." Philippians 1:6. God began a good work in us with our World Championship and with restoring Aria's soundness. He was not going to just toss us aside. He would complete what He started, and returning World could be a platform for Him to showcase this.

Still, I needed Godly counsel on making this decision. I brought up the idea to Teri at Dr. Tolle's, and her face lit up. She was just excited as I was about the possibility of showing the world, literally, what God has done. Dr. Tolle, naturally, focused more on the physical aspect of showing, but did not shoot the idea down. He too became more enthused the more he thought on it. I contacted Mead, knowing, as a horseman and as a Godly man, he would give wise advice. He told me we should go back one more time just because we can and that it is a testimony of how great our God is, though keeping in mind we are not going to try to win the whole thing. I also talked with Daddy and a couple of pastor friends, and the consensus was the same: go back to World to have fun and celebrate what God has done, sharing our story and pointing people to Him. Points did not matter, for I knew it would take a God-sized miracle for us to win again and to earn our remaining points for our register of merit. The results would be entirely up to God and would be whatever would bring Him the most glory. My job was simply to go do our best and savor the moment…and not get disqualified because He sure would not get much glory from that! As for me and Aria, we will serve the LORD. However that looks. However He wants.

God also reminded me that just because the Israelites crossed the Jordan and entered the Promised Land, that did not mean their battles were over. They had actually just begun. Everything in the wilderness prepared them for the battles they still faced. They still had work to do before they could enjoy their Promised Land. The same held true for Aria and me. I had been thinking that we were still in the wilderness every time Aria had a backset, but in reality, those backsets were battles to be fought to enjoy our Promised Land. I realized our Promised Land is not a destination. It is actually a state of mind, of being willing and able to be used by God. Yes, until Aria was sound, we were still in the wilderness, but once she was sound, we became able to be used by God however

He sees fit. Through our testimony. In the show arena. Giving rides to church kids. Our Promised Land has many different facets, no different from that of the Israelites. I just have to listen to see how God wants to use us and when. It is just as important to Him to let one child ride Aria as it is to return to World to proclaim His name and His goodness to all who will listen. Both are aspects of our Promised Land. Both are ways to serve God. Both bring Him joy and glory. It is not about titles or points or placings. It is about the One Who has led us through this and what will encourage others to want to know Him as well.

The time came for me to step out in faith and fill out our entry. I chose to only do Amateur SPB Hunt Seat Equitation. We can use support wraps in that class, and it is also our most confident class. Ranch riding was offered for both amateur and open solids, but because of the scar tissue in Aria's leg, our extended trot is not what it once was, making us less competitive in that class. When I showed in ranch pleasure in June, she tried her best to extend her trot, but when she could not like she used to, she got frustrated, and I could not do that to her again. I did not want to ask too much of Aria either by doing more than one class, especially since they spanned multiple days. We were going in order to bring God glory, and overdoing would not accomplish that in the least. So, I felt like that was God's way of affirming we were to focus on hunt seat equitation.

At the same time, giants started rearing their ugly heads. The giant of choosing the easier way: "we have already won a World Championship in hunt seat equitation...shouldn't we quit while we are ahead?" The giant of pride: "what will people say if we come back to World and fall short?" The giant of fear: "what if we fail miserably and come in last? What if we get disqualified?" The giant of lack of trust: "do You really want us to go back, Lord? Will You really fight for us again? Will You really show up for us again?" One by one God slayed those giants with His truth. It is not about us or our reputation but about Him and His. It is not about how we place but about doing our best to bring Him glory. He will never leave us or forsake us. He will go with us. He will not ask us to do or face anything that He does not already have a plan for how to handle it. We have no reason to fear. He will keep ALL of His promises to us. He reminded me that the results are up to Him. My responsibility is to be obedient and to trust Him.

Originally, I thought the show schedule showed even more of God's orchestration. Our class fell in the afternoon, so with an early start, we would avoid having to spend the night before. I figured Aria would get stiff cooped up in a stall overnight, so God had made sure she would not have to. However, about three weeks before World, I found out about an additional inspection all horses had to go through before being allowed onto the show grounds. A virus was going around, and APHA wanted to prevent it from making an appearance at World in an effort to keep it from spreading. I greatly appreciated that; however, I also envisioned a long line of trailers waiting to be inspected. I realized that could potentially make us miss our class. The safest option would be to haul in the day before to ensure we had plenty of time for the inspection and to get ready to show. Once again, Isaiah 55:8-9 rang true, and God's plan trumped my own. I was trying to cut corners to save money, but God said no. The forced change in plans had caused me a bit of a panic though. No pets were allowed where we had stayed in years past. I was not about to leave Shorty home alone overnight, and there are very few, if any, people Shorty would allow in the house without us there to take care of him. I swear, as I was panicking, God patted me on the head and said, "Google, Sharon. Google." Oh, yeah…good idea, God. So, I googled pet friendly motels near Will Rogers Memorial Center, in Fort Worth, the location of APHA World. Lo, and behold, just down the road was an extended stay motel that allowed dogs up to 3' tall and 3' long. Shorty was well under those limits! God provided yet again! After I started getting used to the idea of hauling in the day before, I also started to see why God's plan was so much better. It would divide the driving between two days instead of doing it all in one. I would not have to worry about being late should we get caught in traffic. While Aria would have to stay the night in the stall, we would have the chance to practice in the arena after classes had ended for the day. This would let Aria take in all the sights and sounds before I needed her undivided attention in our class. Repeatedly, in little ways and big ways, God was showing me His hand in our return to World.

Every day I became more and more overwhelmed by the outpouring of love, support, encouragement, and especially prayers for Aria and me. The intense spiritual warfare around 2017 World had made Mom's absence even more painfully obvious, since she was my prayer warrior who would have fought alongside me, earnestly, in prayer. Friends and family had prayed, but the void was still there. This time it was as if Momma has recruited a whole army to pray in her stead as she bent Jesus's ear in person. Family, friends, both the church I attend and the church where I work, my chiropractor and his staff. Then divine appointments right when I needed an extra dose of affirmation of God's orchestration and of His hand being in this, such as running into Mead at the vet clinic and, at a tack store, crossing paths with her farrier, Leif Martinson, a Godly man who is good friends with Mead and has been an incredible blessing through Aria's recovery and beyond. Both encounters and our conversations provided further affirmation I truly was following the Lord's leading. God kept showing me over and over how people were praying for us and were just as excited about what God was doing as we were.

While this was at the forefront of my mind, I opened up the devotional I was reading, and what I read leapt off the page.[13] It opened with Luke 1:10, "And when the time for burning of incense came, all the assembled worshippers were praying outside." When Zechariah was serving inside the temple, people were praying outside of the temple. That was when an angel appeared to tell him he and his wife Elizabeth would have John the Baptist. People praying outside of a ministry helped bring about incredible things inside of a ministry. Whatever happened at World this time, everyone praying for us would have an important role in helping us bring God glory. People praying outside our ministry would help bring about incredible things inside out ministry. My prayer in return, from outside of their ministry, is that God will show up and move in a mighty way inside their ministry as well.

As I thought more on the differences between 2017 and 2019 World, beyond the most obvious being Aria's leg, God allowed me to see that some of the differences were due to when each show fell in our journey. 2017 World was surrounded by intense, external spiritual warfare because it was our Red Sea crossing. The Israelites were under attack, being pursued by the Egyptian army, when God led them to the Red Sea and brought them victory by decimating the attack on them. At 2017 World, God brought us victory against all odds and defeated the spiritual attacks that were close on our heels by leading me out of the situation. 2019 World is our Jordan River crossing. The spiritual warfare this time is different. Rather than be under attack by external forces around us and behind us, opposition came in the form of internal struggles and the giants ahead of us: fear, pride, the unknown. No one was in pursuit of Israel at the Jordan. Just like ours, their giants they had to battle lay on the other side of the river and in their own hearts as they stood in the very spot their parents and grandparents had caved in fear.

For both 2017 and 2019 the goal was to bring God glory, but this time the desire ran even deeper. In 2017, I wanted people to see how God will help them achieve their dreams, how mighty things happen when He shows up. This time I again prayed He would show up and work in a mighty way, but now to show how He carries us through the tough times and works good from them. To be used by God to share the Gospel – the good news of His grace through Jesus. To show people His restorative power and how He will still use us, scars and all.

A few weeks prior to World we had yet another "get out of the boat" moment. We had been keeping Aria on a small dosage of Bute (an NSAID) to help as she got back into shape. According to APHA rules, she could only be on Bute for five days prior to showing. Periodically through her healing, we had tapered off her Bute, only for something random to happen, and she would have to go back on it. Now, we again had to wean her off of it. I had to leave the comfort of my "Bute Boat" and step onto the waves, trusting that God foresaw all of this when He put us on this path, and He would not have directed us this way had Aria not been able to go without Bute. First, we went from 1g everyday to 1g every other day…and she stayed sound. The weather was hot and humid, even early in the morning, so our rides had to be short due to us both tiring quickly, but still – a week later she was still sound. Then came the day we took her off of the Bute entirely, and again, she remained sound. God was still working miracles! I was overwhelmed by God's goodness to us, though I was still guarded because we had nearly three weeks to go without Bute. We had been through so much, and it was hard to fully believe we were finally coming out of the wilderness, and she was finally going to remain sound. Every ride after she came off the Bute entirely gave me hope what she would, in fact, stay sound. We had stepped out of the boat, and Christ held our hand every step of the way. Thankfully God is understanding and patient with me, constantly reassuring me. Day by day, my fear and apprehension began to fade, to be replaced with His peace, His joy, and confidence in Him.

Two weeks before World, APHA posted the list of class entries. There were to be five in my class. While that number could change between then and when we show, it was not apt to change drastically. I was incredibly grateful for the small class size. That meant there would not be a ton of time waiting around while everyone completed their patterns, as well as not a lot of traffic to contend with during the rail work portion. Our working order would not be finalized until the night before our class in case of any last-minute changes.

As the days counted down, the more surreal it all became. We really were going back to World. God really was orchestrating every step of our journey. We really were going to have the opportunity to testify to the world about what God has done for us. God really was going to use us to bring Himself honor and glory. It truly was hard to fathom. Then the day came when Cherie text me that the patterns had been posted. I was working with Daddy, so I could not immediately look ours up, but I again prayed in earnest that God would fight for us and that the pattern would cater to our strengths, a prayer that I had been praying since entering World. I knew God had led us this far, and He was still going before us. He would not let us down now. Cherie sent me a picture of our pattern, and when I looked at it and read the description, I was absolutely overwhelmed by God's goodness and grace. You see, it was as if the pattern was drawn specifically for us and for Aria's abilities. I could not have asked for a more perfect pattern if I had been able to draw it myself. God had shown up and moved in a mighty way behind the scenes, yet again. He was ensuring we had every possible chance of bringing Him glory. It was now up to us to make the most of them. It was time to practice the elements of the pattern individually and then together as a whole so that the pattern would flow as effortlessly as possible, and we could be confident and relaxed, trusting God's plan.

I quickly discovered Aria's paddock was too small and too uneven to be able to practice the pattern as a whole. At first I was frustrated, fearing if I could not practice the pattern in its entirety, I was setting myself up for failure and for letting God down, not to mention letting everyone down who has been cheering us on and praying for us. Like in my moment of panic about finding a place to stay that would allow me to bring Shorty, God allowed me to take a beat, patiently waiting for me to pull myself together and look to Him for guidance. At that point, I was able to see that I could divide the pattern up into thirds: ride the first portion, then move to where the land was conducive to riding the next portion, and then do the same to ride the final portion. God sure knew what He was doing when He gave me that idea, because not only did we get to practice all that would be required, in the order it was required, having to ride it in sections slowed the pace down, keeping Aria from anticipating and me from getting into a rush trying to make the whole thing fit in a small spot. A rushed pattern is not a pretty pattern, and you cannot have a beautiful performance without beautiful practice.

God even provided an opportunity to work on the pattern in an arena the week before World. Even though I could not afford lessons, Tracey had graciously offered to let us haul to her place to ride in her arena, but every time I thought we would have the chance, something would come up, and it would be impossible. Knowing how God had been guiding every step of the way, I knew there had to be a reason for this, even though I may never know exactly what that reason was. So, I just accepted that it was not meant to be. Once when I was talking to Mead at one of our chance encounters at Dr. Tolle's, Mead said he would be happy to work with us on our pattern once it was posted. He had located an arena that would let me haul in, so as soon as I had the pattern, I sent it to him, and he was still more than willing to get together to school Aria. This time everything fell into place. We were able to meet up a couple of times before we left for World, and we picked apart the pattern, working on pieces of it rather than the pattern as a whole in order to keep Aria from learning to anticipate what she was supposed to do. Being able to learn from Mead was such a blessing. He gave us valuable pointers, as well as some much-needed encouragement. He commented on how much more focused Aria was compared to when he had worked with us at Sam and Michelle's a few years prior. He also said she was even moving better than before, too. She was driving from behind very well and carrying herself "flatter," meaning her head and neck were lower and more relaxed. After all that she had been through, for her to actually look better and behave better was truly another miracle. God knew how important it was for me to hear that, so it all made sense then why He ensured we met up with Mead rather than Tracey.

God had been and was still orchestrating our path, and His presence felt just as tangible as it had in 2017. He went before us then, fighting for us, and He was continuing to do so in 2019. Seeing this was incredibly exciting and filled me with peace at the same time, that no matter what happened, no matter how we placed, God was going to use it for good and for His glory.

I was once again reminded of Momma's favorite verse, Deuteronomy 31:8, and the significance of that verse really hit home, not just what it says, but the circumstances around it. Moses said this to Joshua as Israel was preparing to enter the Promised Land. Moses knew he would not be able to enter the land with Joshua and the Israelites, so he was offering hope and encouragement as he passed the torch of leadership to Joshua, reminding him of God's abiding presence, God's orchestration and leading, and God's perfect comfort and peace. Momma knew that there would come a point when she would be unable to continue with me in the journey towards the Promised Land God has for me. Therefore, like Moses, she instilled in me the hope and promise of her favorite verse, to trust that promise, even once she was no longer with me. The lessons she taught me have lived on after her, and I knew she would again be cheering us on in Heaven, alongside countless other loved ones. I smiled at that thought, and then I smiled a bit bigger when I thought about how since us returning to World was all by God's hand, Jesus Himself would be in that cheering section, too.

Points to Ponder...

- What pieces are falling together for you so that you can see God's orchestration in your circumstances?

- What promises has God brought to mind to affirm His will? Who has He used to provide further affirmation and how?

- How has God changed your perspective of yourself and your situation as you near your Promised Land?

Chapter 16

To God Be the Glory

"The LORD has done great things for us and we are filled with joy."
Psalm 126:3

As planned, we hauled into Fort Worth for World the day before we were to show. We got inspected and checked in rather quickly. I was able to get stalls out of the way of most of the foot traffic to give Aria and Shorty both some peace and quiet. Like at the Margarita Classic, we had a cable for Shorty and secured him to the base of the stall wall. This allowed him freedom, but not so much that he would go visiting other folks. While Daddy got the stall ready for Aria, putting down mats and shavings, I unloaded the trailer. Aria hung out in what would be the tack stall during all this, and Shorty supervised all of us. He did remarkably well the whole time at the show. He would cry when I would leave him to get another load, but never once did he get upset at anyone walking by. He would greet everyone as if they were old friends. Even golf carts going by did not bother him, which is highly unusual, for he typically barks at four-wheelers, ATVs, and the like. Other dogs would run up to him, and he would just sniff and wiggle. Even a loose horse wandered by at one point, and he just watched it go by. I could not be more proud of how Shorty acted. Once Aria was settled into her stall and all our tack and gear safely stowed away, I checked the practice schedule. The arena was not going to be open until after 10pm, so we had plenty of time to get settled in the motel, eat supper, cool off, and rest up a bit.

When we got back, I tacked up Aria, and the plan was to leave Shorty in the tack stall. Aria and I left to practice, and Daddy waited out of sight to see if Shorty calmed down. I rode Aria into the arena, and it was teeming with other horses. In the past, Aria would have been overwhelmed by all the traffic and melted down. This time, she acted like a seasoned pro. We warmed up, dodging horses, dogs, and people. She felt great! Relaxed, driving from behind, focused. I was careful to work her both directions so that should could take in all the sights and sounds from each way. Once the arena cleared enough, we even ran through our pattern as a whole. I was thrilled with how she was doing. We worked on a couple of rough spots in our pattern to smooth them out, and then as I rounded the corner, I looked up, and who was sitting in the stands but Daddy…and Shorty!! When I made eye contact with Shorty, he leaped to his feet and started wiggling all over and started yipping. It was so precious! I was a bit concerned his calling out to me would upset people, but no one seemed to care. I found out later Shorty just would not settle down, so Daddy brought Shorty with him to watch. They had both been there the whole time! I was so impressed Shorty had watched patiently for that long.

I felt confident after our practice, but I also took note that the longer Aria and I worked, the more excited she got. I knew that the next day I would need to walk a fine line with her to get her warm and relaxed and not let her get hot and bothered. She would be much easier to show if I did. I checked the working order, and we were to go third. I had been hoping to go first so that we would not have to wait at all to do our pattern, but third was much better than being last. God had orchestrated everything thus far. I just had to trust that this was part of His plan, too.

The next morning, we fed Aria, and for a time she seemed content. That did not last long. She started getting mad, striking the stall door, pacing, biting at the stall walls. Even Shorty being right by her stall did not calm her down. All I could do was tack her up and take her up to the warm-up pen to see if that would help. As soon as she started to work, Aria calmed down and focused. I rode her for a while, and then I decided it was time to take her back to the stall for a water break. I was remembering the fine line I had to walk when practicing to keep her from getting worked up, so I did not want to overdo it. It was still early in the day. Back in the stall, she gulped her water down happily and started munching on hay, but again, that did not last long. I decided to just go ahead and braid her and get dressed so that if I had to stay in the warm-up arena until our class, and just walk back and forth for water, I could. When I pulled her out of the stall and started braiding her, she began to relax a bit. She must have been getting claustrophobic in the stall. While I was braiding Aria, my cousin Debbie Moore and her daughter Wendy arrived. Debbie and Aria had not seen each other in years, but I could tell Aria remembered her. Seeing them together again was such a tender moment amongst all the chaos. We all trekked up to the warm-up pen, Shorty, too, so that Aria would stay calm. Shorty did well, except he kept trying to crawl through the panels around the arena to get to Aria and me, so he ended up having to go back to the tack stall. He cried for a bit, but eventually settled down when he realized that even though he was alone, he was still surrounded by Aria's and my gear, so we would be back.

The time finally came to check in with the equipment judge. I had planned to ride Aria in her support wraps since in the equipment chart in rulebook said they were allowed for jumping, equitation over fences, and equitation on the flat. Hunt Seat Equitation was the only flat class I knew of that was an equitation class, so I thought we were good. I knew, however, that elsewhere in the rulebook it said support wraps were only allowed in jumping. Because of the discrepancy, I was prepared for the equipment judge to say the wraps were not allowed, which was exactly what happened. I did not argue and just complied and took off her wraps. As I walked her around in the paddock waiting for the rest of the class to check in, I began to pray in earnest for God's protection. We had ridden without wraps occasionally because I knew this situation was a distinct possibility, but riding at home without them was very different than riding without them at World when both Aria's and my adrenaline was flowing.

As we walked down the ramp towards the arena, the gravity of the moment truly sunk in. After all we had been through, we were about to once again compete against top riders from across the nation, from across the continent. Tears welled as I thought on what all God had done. As I waited at the gate for our turn, the gate keeper was giving me directions, and I could tell by the look on her face, she could see I was emotional. So, I quickly told her our story. She about broke down herself and said, "you are supposed to be here." That last second affirmation was God's way of giving me one last measure of peace before our pattern began.

Aria, as usual, did not want to stand still as we waited just inside the arena, but once the ring steward signaled for us to begin, she was all business. She walked off smartly, but broke to a trot for a step or two before the cone that marked where we were supposed to begin trotting. I quickly quieted her back down to a walk, and this time she waited for my cue to trot off to the center of the arena. When we reached the center, she stopped promptly and squarely, and she turned on her forehand to the left precisely, responding to just a light touch of my leg. She cantered off without missing a beat, performing a lovely, round half circle, a perfectly straight line across the arena, and a tight turn to the right to cut across the arena diagonally. She was so enthused about cantering, she resisted returning to the trot at first, but then submitted. At center we began cantering again, this time making a tight turn to the left to go straight across the arena. Both tight turns, she bent her body around the turn, making it look effortless, even though I knew it took a lot of strength on her part to keep cantering as she turned. Her ability to turn well came in handy again as we made a 90 degree turn at the canter towards the final portion of our pattern. We came to a halt just before center, and she stopped so hard, her rump tucked underneath her, and she almost slid. When I asked her to back, she dropped her head, rounded her neck and back, and briskly moved in reverse. She was moving so well, I let her back for several steps to show her off. We were to then turn on the haunch to the right to exit the arena, and she rolled over her hocks so quickly that it caught me by surprise. I felt like I was riding a reining rollback. She had never pivoted that fast before! I grinned from ear to ear thinking, "Mead is going to love that!" As I sat the trot out of the arena, I just let the joy wash over me. I did not even try to stem the tears. We had just performed a beautiful pattern at the APHA World Show. I knew it was not perfect, but I knew we had done our best, performing our pattern as an act of worship, testifying to the greatness of God, which was the whole purpose behind our return to World.

The time between our pattern and the rail portion gave me the opportunity to share what God had done for us with the other riders, while Aria caught her breath. One seemed to choke up as she shared her own story of her journey to World. Without divulging details, she too confessed she had faced adversity and just being at World was a huge accomplishment for her as well. We walked our horses around the small holding pen to keep them loose as we waited for the signal to return to the arena. When the time came, we all trotted into the arena like we were playing follow the leader. Aria was wanting to trot faster than the other horses, so rather than fight with her, I let her move to the inside and pass them. As she did, she stretched down, flattening out just like Mead had recommended. As we approached the end of our first lap, the announcer asked us to walk, and then shortly after to halt. At that moment, a ring steward got my attention, tipped his hat, and excused us from the arena, no explanation given. I was shocked. As I walked out the gate, I looked for someone to tell me what happened. No one said. The equipment judge who had checked us in was on break and down in the holding pen talking to the steward who had let us know when to go into the arena. I asked if they had seen what happened, and they did not. All they could figure was if we were excused from the rail, Aria had to have been short-strided or lame. I was crushed. Devastated in fact. Tears poured for an entirely different reason as I made the long walk back to the barn. I had not felt anything wrong. Questions flooded my mind. What had happened? How in the world did this bring God glory? He had brought us back to World. He orchestrated our path. Why would He do that knowing the outcome would be disqualification? None of this made sense.

I put Aria back in her stall. Her getting mad about it was the least of my worries at this point. Daddy was the first one back to the barn. I just collapsed in his arms in tears. Debbie and Wendy were close behind. Everyone was devastated. No one had seen a reason for us to be disqualified. I knew the vet clinic had blocked off the time to watch our class on the live feed, so I quickly fired a message to Teri to see if she saw any sign of lameness or what had happened. She had been watching and had also videoed the whole class on her phone so that they would be able to re-watch it later. She had not seen anything. Dr. Tolle watched as well, and he said she was obviously in a hurry, but he did not see any lameness. Relief washed over me knowing she was okay, even though I still had no clue what we had done to warrant disqualification. Mead called when I told him the results, and he was just as heartbroken as the rest of us. None of it made sense. He suggested trying to look at the score sheets and talking to the show office to see if they knew why we were disqualified. Debbie and Wendy had to leave, but I promised to let them know if I found anything out. Daddy started getting ready to pack up and haul out as I tried to track down answers. I did not get any. The score sheets would not be available until probably the next day, and because of that, the show office knew nothing. I ran into one of the other riders who had also been disqualified, but for making a grievous error in her pattern, who said she had heard rumor our disqualification was due to lameness, and when I told them my vet had been watching and saw no signs of lameness, she was just as confused as I was. She promised to send me pictures of the score sheets once they were posted.

I could not wrap my head around what had just happened. We did all we could do. I had done my best to make sure everything was for God's glory and not for mine, and yet I had somehow failed. At least I felt like it. In my mind, our disqualification brought God dishonor instead of honor. I had envisioned placing well, maybe even winning a second World Championship, and being able to say, "look what God did! He took what was broken and used us to bring about a victory in His name!" But that was not what happened at all. How was I supposed to tell people what happened? How would they respond? What would they think of God because of my failure? I had so many more questions than answers, and I knew everyone who had been praying for us would have questions, too.

Shorty and Aria both knew something was wrong, but they did not know what. Daddy went to go get the trailer while I got everything ready to load. I tried to clean out the tack stall planning to move Aria over there while I pulled up the mats, but I could not keep her calm and pack. I discovered the only way to keep her calm was to be in the stall with her and scratch her back. After a few minutes she relaxed. She let me pull up all the duct tape off the mats and stack them with her just calmly walking around the stall, moving out of the way as needed. Shorty kept his nose to the crack of the stall door keeping an eye on things because he knew Big Sister had been angry earlier, and he was poised to fuss at her if needed to help me out. With me in the stall, Aria was herself, even climbing on top of the pile of mats like she was playing queen of the mountain. Now, looking back, she needed my presence to have peace, just like I needed God's presence in that moment to have peace in amongst all the doubt, uncertainty, despair, and shattered dreams. Once Daddy returned with the trailer, we packed up and hauled out.

The whole way home I wrestled with what to say on social media about what had happened. I knew many of my family and friends had watched the live feed, and I was sure they were just as confused and as devastated as we were. I knew they deserved answers, but I wanted to make sure my answers brought peace to the situation instead of stirring the pot. It would be easy to get angry and point fingers and cast blame. I also knew the "arm-chair vets" would be out in force. I knew my supporters would rally around us, but I also feared that there might be those who would pounce on the opportunity to tear us down. The main thing was I did not want anyone to think God had failed us. I had made it clear that God had orchestrated our path back to World, and I knew I needed to frame my "official statement" to make it clear that while I was at a loss for why things happened like they did, God did not abandon us or set us up to fail. He does not do that. Ever. I had to show people the good from our experience and help them look past the bad. Mainly because if I could help them do that, then I could help myself do the same. I prayed in earnest for God to give me the words to say as well as peace and understanding.

Gradually, God impressed upon me that while World did not go at all like I had hoped, in a way, it actually did. Aria did everything I had asked her to do. We successfully completed our pattern in the World Show arena. Some parts were just acceptable, but others were fantastic. I knew beyond a shadow of a doubt that God had orchestrated our path back to World. My goal had been for us to have a performance that would honor God and bring Him glory. When I trotted out of that arena, beaming with tears of joy, praising her and so proud of her, I knew in my heart of hearts we had done just that. It did not matter what the judges thought. What mattered was that we gave it our best effort. What mattered the most was what God thought of us. He impressed upon me that maybe He allowed us to be disqualified and not complete the rail portion because Aria did not need to work that hard, that long without the support of her wraps. Maybe He was actually protecting us. The results of our class were not at all what I had hoped for, but in a way, they were still what I had prayed for. While it was clear God wanted us there, my prayer had been that the results would bring the most glory to Him, however that looked. With the resulting disqualification, He is the only one who gets glory because I sure do not. My performance may have somehow kept me from getting accolades, but He still gets the glory for healing my precious Aria, and I was still able to testify to those with whom I came in contact about what He has done for us. Good would come from this still though. God promises that.

Once we were home, and Aria was settled in at the barn, I took a deep breath and wrote my post. The videographer had emailed me the link to the video of our pattern, so I shared that as well. What happened next was not what I expected. Messages and comments of love and support and understanding came flooding in. As heartbroken as I was, there was comfort knowing they shared my heartbreak. Countless people watched and analyzed our pattern, trying to spot what the judges saw that would cause them to disqualify us. Honestly, I think more people watched our performance because of our DQ than would have watched it if we had won. I realized then, that maybe that was the good coming from all of this. More people were seeing what God had done, His healing and His grace, than would have otherwise. A majority of the horsemen and women who watched our pattern were very complimentary. After Mead had time to review the video of our class, and study it closely, we talked again. He was absolutely thrilled with our pattern, especially with the halt, back, and turn on the haunch sequence, just like I had guessed he would. He assured me that we did an excellent job, and Aria and I had looked fantastic. Knowing he was proud of us and of our pattern, that brought joy to my weary soul. I knew in that moment I had not failed God. I had in fact ridden a pattern that brought Him glory. No one could pinpoint anything that was worthy of disqualification though. Of course, there were a couple of vocal critics, but I also knew to consider the source and take it in stride.

Days passed and the outpouring of encouragement continued. I kept waiting on the other rider to send me pictures of the score sheets as promised, but they never arrived. A friend of mine showing the following week gladly stopped by the show office and took pictures of the score sheets for me. One of the five judges had written "lame" by our score, so all any of us could figure was that in that short time we were on the rail, that judge saw something he or she considered a sign of lameness and erred on the side of caution. The incredible part was, though, when I tallied all of the judges' scores, if we had not been DQ'd, we would have placed third!! After all Aria had been through, she still scored well enough to have placed third in the world! I was floored and overwhelmed by God's grace. Even though we have no ribbon or prizes to show for it, I will always have that knowledge. God had indeed shown up for us yet again at World. We never have figured out what the judge saw, but that is okay. Granted, the results were not at all what I had wanted or what any of us thought would happen, but our return to World was not about prizes or trophies or titles or points anyway. It was about honoring God and what He has done for us. It was about bringing Him glory. My prayer is that through all of this, the good and the bad, we have still accomplished that.

"He has made everything beautiful in its time." Ecclesiastes 3:11a. In His time. In His time, God has taken this difficult path, full of hardship and heartache, and made something beautiful from it. He took a small-town girl with big dreams and her beautiful mare and made them World Champions. He took a devastating injury and made it a testimony of His grace, healing, and restoring power. He brought us back to the APHA World Show to prove that He can still do the impossible. He took our broken pieces and created something more beautiful, more amazing than I could have ever imagined. God showed up in our lives and worked miracles, and He will do the same for you.

Points to Ponder...

- When outcomes do not line up with your expectations, how do you respond? How does God work to shift your focus off the outcome and back onto Him?

- How have you seen God use the outcome you did not expect to bring Himself glory anyways? How did He use it for good after all?

- What lessons have you learned from your wilderness journey that have changed your life and deepened your faith? How will you apply these lessons in the days ahead as you continue into your Promised Land?

Joe and Annell Witherspoon around 1979 or 1980

Momma and I when I received my Midway College IHSA team jacket.

Momma and I on the Midway College campus

Momma and I at IHSA Regionals, Sewanee, Tennessee, sophomore year. She is holding the note of encouragement that she and Daddy wrote to me and put in the show program.

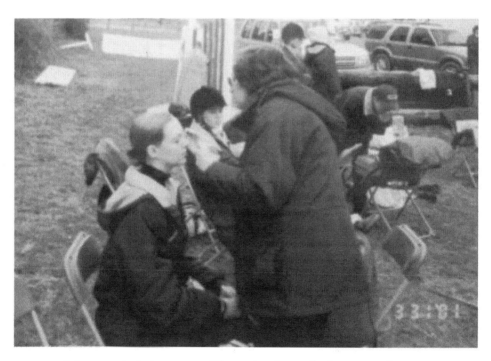

Momma helping me with my makeup before my class.

Momma and Daddy
with Aria when she
was almost three
months old.

August 2001

Aria's first ride. Camp El Har, Dallas, Texas. Summer 2003

(Above)

Blue as a puppy and I
in the bluebonnets.

Spring 2004

(Left)

Blue as an adult and I
in the bluebonnets.

Spring 2011

Blue and her dragon. She loved to play. She always took great care of her toys. The only toy she ever destroyed was an "indestructible" firehose, most likely just to prove she could. All of her stuffed animals she would love on them, groom them, and throw them around, but she would never hurt them.

February 2012

Aria and Blue.

When Blue was just a puppy, Aria chased her out of the pasture. After that, Blue would not get close to her. This was as close as she would get, and that was only because Blue knew the fence would keep Aria away from her.

September 2014

Momma and I on a trail ride together. She is riding Stetson, a gelding I adopted from Camp El Har. Stetson was a great horse, trustworthy, kind, and a complete joy to ride. He enjoyed his retirement years with Aria.

April 2006

Stetson, Daddy, Momma, my brother, Thomas, and Aria and I.
Loy Lake Open Horse Show, Denison, Texas, April 2006

Daddy, Aria, and I at my truck and trailer.
Horseman's Association of Texoma (HAT) Open Show
Bonham, Texas, May 2011

Aria and I posing amongst the buttercups after a HAT Open Show in Bonham, Texas

April 2011

Momma and I visiting with family at a HAT Open Show, April 2012.
This was the last show Momma was able to attend.

Circle J Cowboy Church Open Show, Collinsville, Texas, May 2011

North Central Texas College Open Show, Gainesville, Texas, April 2013

On multiple occasions, Aria and I were given the honor of carrying the flag for the National Anthem at HAT Open Shows Bonham, Texas.

Our bond and trust in each other allows us
to ride bareback and bridleless.

Momma and Daddy
on their
40th anniversary,
April 29, 2012.

Daddy, Momma, Me, and Blue, celebrating their 40th anniversary.
Photo taken by my brother, Thomas.

My sweet friend
Larinda Smith took
these portraits of Aria,
Blue, and me for
Momma's Christmas
present.

2011

I love this mare
so much.

Left photo by
Larinda Smith

November 2011

Below taken by
Daddy

February 2015

Aria and I jumping our homemade bucket oxer, practicing over fences at home.

February 2013

Aria and I jumping our vertical that Daddy and I built ourselves.

September 2013

Jumping lesson Spellbound Farm Van Alstyne, Texas

March 2014

(Above and left)

Aria's and my first APHA show, hosted by the Permian Basin Paint Horse Club, held at El Lobo Ranch in Gainesville, Texas.

September 2014

Paint Performance Horse Super Stakes Club Show, Gainesville, July 2015

Permian Basin Paint Horse Club Show, Gainesville, September 2015

One of my friends captured this picture of Daddy videoing my
class so that Momma could watch it when we got home.
Our dream of winning a World Championship only came true
because God blessed me with such an incredible father. We
could not have done it without him. I am so grateful for him.

This photo was taken by the Paint Horse Journal during our victory gallop. They posted it on the APHA Facebook page during World, and later they used it with the article Alana Harrison wrote about us.
This is the picture Bill Douglass had hung in our local gas station.
(Rights purchased by author from Larry Williams Photography who sold them on behalf of the PHJ)

(Above)

2017 World Champions Amateur
Solid Paint Bred
Hunt Seat Equitation

Awards presented by APHA Executive Committee Member Karen Thomas.

(Left)

Daddy, me, Aria, and Tracey Badley Walton, Spellbound Farm's owner and trainer.

Our trophy buckle by Gist Silversmiths.

Being interviewed by Kristin Weaver for KXII News.
Photo taken by Tracey Badley Walton at Spellbound Farm.

(Counterclockwise)

Aria and I walking over logs at
the beginning of our
SPB Ranch Riding pattern.

Aria and I extending our trot.

My dear friend Cherie Bugg
and her horse, Barbie

Stepping up to receive our awards for 3rd place in SPB Ranch Riding.

The always entertaining,
absolutely adorable
Shorty.
Words cannot express what a
blessing he is. I am forever
grateful God orchestrated his
steps to bring him to me.

Unlike Blue, Shorty adores Aria and
loves spending time with her .

(Above left)

Family Portrait taken by Daddy
April 2018

(Above)

Shorty playing tug of war with Aria,
who was more concerned with grazing.
April 2018

(Left)

Shorty and Aria seem to be laughing at
a really good joke.
July 2018

Shorty's favorite pastime while Aria and I are riding is chasing grasshoppers. As you can see, Shorty can hop as well as they can!

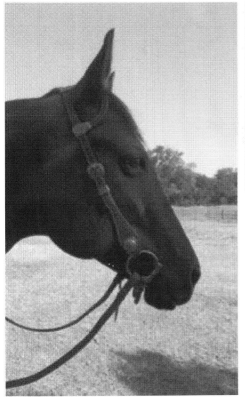

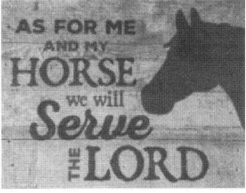

No matter what the future holds for Aria and me, God still has a plan to use us to bring Him honor and glory. Our mission in life will always be what the above plaque says. This hangs on the wall with Aria's ribbons.

(Above)

Shorty was a rock star at his first horse show, even impressing folks who walked by as he sat in my lap while I ate my lunch.

(Right)

The smile says it all.

Margarita Classic
Waco, Texas
November 2018

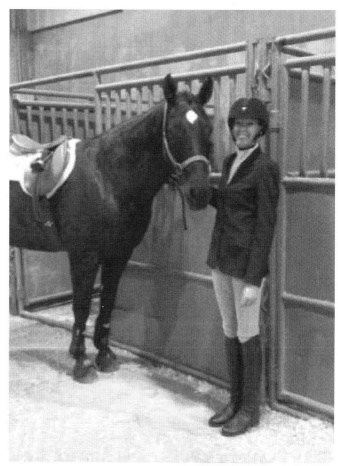

Shorty is always
more than ready
for a truck ride.
He was elated to
go with us to
2019 APHA
World.

Shorty behaved perfectly in the barn at 2019 World.

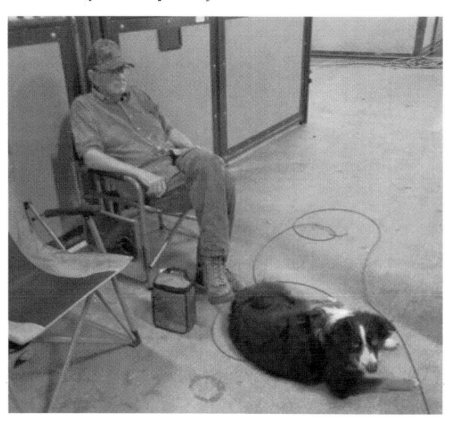

Daddy and I discussing how Aria was doing. (Above)
Aria and I trying to remain relaxed before our class. (Below)
Photo credit: Wendy Moore, September 17, 2019

Warming up prior to our class. (Above)
Waiting at the gate for our turn to perform our pattern. (Below)
Photo credit: Wendy Moore, September 17, 2019

Performing our pattern in Am SPB Hunt Seat Equitation. (Above)
Trotting our lap during the rail portion of the class. (Below)
Photo credit: Wendy Moore, September 17, 2019

Notes

1 Holly Gerth, *You're Made for a God-Sized Dream*, (Grand Rapids: Revell, 2013).

2 Priscilla Shirer, *The Armor of God,* (Nashville: LifeWay Press, 2015).

3 Josh Groban, *You Raise Me Up*, Songwriters: Brendan Graham/Rolf Loveland, Peermusic Publishing, 2003.

4 Oswald Chambers, "What My Obedience to God Costs Other People," *My Utmost for His Highest*, (Grand Rapids: Discovery House Publishers, 1992), January 11.

5 *Great Is Thy Faithfulness*, Songwriters: Thomas O. Chisholm/William M. Runyan, Hope Publishing, 1923, renewed 1951.

6 Priscilla Shirer, *The Armor of God,* (Nashville: LifeWay Press, 2015), 57.

7 Mahatma Gandhi, as quoted by *goodreads* (online), cited 13 March 2018. Available on the Internet: *goodreads.com.*

8 Billy Graham, posted on Billy Graham's *Facebook,* 26 August 2011.

9 Kristen Weaver, "Horseback Rider from Bells Wins World Championship Competition," *KXII News*, 27 September 2017. Available on the Internet: http://www.kxii.com/content/news/Horseback-rider-from-Bells-wins-world-championship-competition-448341793.html.

[10] Alana Harrison, "Member Profile," *Paint Horse Journal,* (Fort Worth: American Paint Horse Association, December 2017), 44.

[11] Priscilla Shirer, *The Armor of God,* (Nashville: LifeWay Press, 2015), 114-115.

[12] Matthew West, *Broken Things,* Songwriters: Matthew West/Jason C. Houser/Andrew Jacob Pruis, Amplified Administration, 2017.

[13] Priscilla Shirer, "Day 67: Ins and Outs of Prayer," *Awaken,* (Nashville: B&H Publishing Group, 2018), 271-272.

Made in the USA
Coppell, TX
10 March 2020